Sound Bites

Pronunciation Activities

Joann Rishel Kozyrev

Houghton Mifflin Company   Boston   New York

Publisher: Patricia A. Coryell
Director, ESL Publishing: Susan Maguire
Development Editor: Kathy Sands-Boehmer
Editorial Assistant: Evangeline Bermas
Associate Project Editor: Shelley Dickerson
Senior Manufacturing Coordinator: Marie Barnes
Marketing Manager: Annamarie Rice
Marketing Associate: Laura Hemrika

Cover image: © 2003 Joseph Sherman, Sound Bites

Printed in the U.S.A.

Library of Congress Control Number: 2002109498

ISBN: 0-618-25972-4

123456789–CRS–08 07 06 05 04

Contents

I love to teach pronunciation. I love it because my students have always loved to improve their pronunciation. They will work at it for hours, and beg for it to be included in classes because they know without being told that pronunciation is the "face" of their spoken English. It is the first thing that their listeners notice. The exercises in *Sound Bites* were created to help students learn about English pronunciation in a fun and engaging way.

Whether you are an experienced teacher of pronunciation or a novice, you can use *Sound Bites* to plan and teach useful, interactive pronunciation lessons. Each chapter is designed to be taught in a single class session. Of course, it may take a little more time if the material is challenging for the students, or it make take a little less time if the students do the listening exercises for homework. I would like to offer a few suggestions for teaching with this book.

1. Don't go through the book chapters in numerical order. Instead, choose the chapters that your students need the most. The diagnostic quiz and the sample syllabus on the *Sound Bites* instructor's website (**college.hmco.com/esl/instructors/**) are there to help you with your choices.

2. Try to alternate between teaching suprasegmental features (which are covered in Parts 1, 2, and 5) and covering the individual sounds (in Parts 3 and 4).

3. Remind students to focus on the pronunciation feature covered in each chapter. Sometimes students get so involved in the act of communicating that they forget that the primary goal of the lessons is to practice their pronunciation. For more ideas on helping students to monitor their progress, see the *Sound Bites* instructor's website.

4. Remember that change takes time and remind the students (and yourself) that you are teaching them *what* they need to change and *how* they can do it. However, they must take responsibility for the daily practice that will be required to make the change a permanent part of their speech.

5. Aim for comprehensible speech. Students should make it their goal to be understood by most listeners, not to eliminate their accent. Having a memorable, easy-to-understand accent can be a real asset in life.

I hope you enjoy teaching with *Sound Bites*.

Best wishes,
Joann Rishel Kozyrev

I want you to be proud of your accent when you speak English. Having a unique accent tells people a little bit about you and where you are from. It also helps people to remember you, and that can be a real advantage. Of course, your accent is only an advantage if people can understand you easily. To make your accent understandable, you will have to do four things:

1. Find out what your biggest problems are. Your teacher can help you do this. You can use the chart on page ix to make a record of these problems.

2. Practice listening to examples of correct pronunciation. In fact, practice listening to English as much as you can.

3. Practice speaking correctly. You must do this every day. See the *Sound Bites* student website for ideas for daily practice.

4. Listen to your own speech. Are you speaking correctly? A tape recorder can help you listen to your speech, but you can also teach your ear to hear your mistakes, and you can even teach your tongue to "feel wrong" when you make a sound incorrectly.

I hope that the practice you get while using *Sound Bites* helps you to make your accent one that you are proud of!

Good Luck!
Joann Rishel Kozyrev

Acknowledgments

First, and foremost, I am indebted to Susan Maguire, for she gave me the chance to write this book. This is just one of the many doors of opportunity that Susan has opened for me, and I am thankful to have benefited from her experience and creativity. This is the book I have wanted to write ever since I was in graduate school at Penn State. I am grateful to Dr. Patricia Dunkel, Dr. Karen Johnson, and Dr. Anne Lazarton, who were on my committee and helped to shape my master's paper on Communicative Pronunciation Exercises.

I feel privileged to work with Kathy Sands-Boehmer, who is always a source of comfort, encouragement, and excellent ideas, not just for me, but for all of her authors. I also wish to thank Annamarie Rice who is a source of support and never hesitates to help when asked. Jane Sturtevant provided valuable suggestions that shaped this book in its early stages, and I could not have completed this project without the excellent advice and guidance of Angela Castro. Alisa Ochoa kindly agreed to create the playful images which appear at the beginning of each of the five parts of the book. I am also grateful to Cindy Johnson for her patience and skill in guiding this book through the production process.

I was very fortunate to have received exceptionally good advice and suggestions from the following ESL instructors who reviewed Sound Bites in various stages of its development:

Karin Avila-John, *University of Dayton*

Mary DiStefano-Diaz, *Broward Community College*

Timothy Ely, *Delaware County Community College*

Robert Giron, *Montgomery College*

Shelley Robinson, *PACE University*

Hollis Shaw, *Houston Community College*

Gay Washburn, *Syracuse University*

Use this chart to make a note of what pronunciation features you need to practice to make your English more understandable. You can keep a record of your progress by checking off each of the four goals as you reach them.

Pronunciation Features	Goal 1: I understand how to make this pronunciation feature.	Goal 2: I can hear this when I listen carefully.	Goal 3: I pronounce this correctly when I am thinking about it and try to do it right.	Goal 4: I pronounce this correctly most of the time.

1. These pronunciation features make it difficult for others to understand me. I should work on them first.

_____ _____ _____ _____ _____

_____ _____ _____ _____ _____

_____ _____ _____ _____ _____

_____ _____ _____ _____ _____

2. These features are sometimes a problem for me. I will work on them once I've begun to make progress on Group 1.

_____ _____ _____ _____ _____

_____ _____ _____ _____ _____

_____ _____ _____ _____ _____

_____ _____ _____ _____ _____

3. These features are interesting to me, but are not a big problem. I will work on them if I have time.

_____ _____ _____ _____ _____

_____ _____ _____ _____ _____

_____ _____ _____ _____ _____

_____ _____ _____ _____ _____

Using a Dictionary to Improve Your Pronunciation

A good dictionary is very useful for pronunciation improvement. A dictionary has tools you can use to learn how to pronounce new words. These practice activities will help you make a habit of using your dictionary's pronunciation guides.

Using a dictionary to find the correct syllable stress for a new word

In Chapter 2 of *Sound Bites*, you learn about syllable stress. Incorrect syllable stress is one of the most common pronunciation mistakes that learners make. Check a dictionary when you learn a new word, and you can be sure to get it right the first time.

1. The example word, *pronounce*, has two syllables, and the second syllable is stressed. Some dictionaries mark the stress by putting an accent mark after the stressed syllable.

> pro nounce'

Other dictionaries mark the stress by putting an accent mark before the stressed syllable.

> pro'nounce

In *Sound Bites*, syllable stress is marked by writing the stressed syllable in capital letters:

> proNOUNCE

Look up the word *pronounce* in your dictionary. Write it on the line below and mark the stress in the same way that your dictionary does.

_____

2. Look up these words in your dictionary. First, divide the words into syllables. Then, mark the stressed syllable.

1. data
2. economy
3. illegal
4. individual
5. insignificantly
6. percent
7. respond
8. specifically

3. Write six words that you want to learn to pronounce correctly. Then, look up the words in your dictionary. Divide each word into syllables, and mark the stressed syllable.

1. _____   4. _____

2. _____   5. _____

3. _____   6. _____

Using a dictionary to find out how a word sounds

Inside the front cover of *Sound Bites* you will see a guide that shows the symbols this book uses to show each of the sounds of the English language. Dictionaries also use a system like this. However, each dictionary uses a different system, and each has a pronunciation guide to help you learn to pronounce words correctly.

1. Find the pronunciation guide in your dictionary. What page is it on? _____

Write the symbol(s) that your dictionary uses for each English sound next to the same sound on the chart inside the front cover of this book.

2. Look up these words in your dictionary to find the correct pronunciation. Use the symbols in your dictionary to pronounce the words to a partner or make an audio recording of your pronunciation of these words. Check with your teacher to see if you read the pronunciation symbols in your dictionary correctly.

1. analyze   5. method

2. identify   6. section

3. involve   7. source

4. major   8. theory

3. Write six words that you want to learn to pronounce correctly. Then, look up the words in your dictionary and use the pronunciation guide to learn to pronounce the words. Record your pronunciation of these words or pronounce them for a partner.

1. _____   4. _____

2. _____   5. _____

3. _____   6. _____

Use this space to record notes about your pronunciation. You might list words that you want to learn to say with the syllable stress and pronunciation marked. Perhaps you will write down something you heard a native speaker say in an unfamiliar way so that you can ask your teacher or a friend about it.

Examples:

ar / e / a (3 syllables)

"You coming with us." Oscar said this like a question. Why
did he use rising intonation?

Learning the rhythm of English is the best way to quickly make your English more understandable. To improve your rhythm, you will first learn about syllables and syllable stress, which are the basis for English rhythm. Be sure to study these chapters carefully. Your teacher will probably ask you to study the first few chapters in Part One, and then come back to the other chapters in Part One after practicing other pronunciation skills in other parts of the book.

Tip

In addition to studying the rules for stress and rhythm, you can improve the rhythm of your speech by listening to the rhythm of English. Listen to audio or video recordings of English speakers as often as you can, and listen to the rhythm as though you are listening to music. You may also find that it helps you to learn the stress pattern of a word or phrase if you tap your fingers or nod your head to emphasize the rhythm as you say it. These tips will help you learn rhythm from the inside.

Chapter 1
Syllables

Every English word has one or more syllables. A syllable is a part of a word. The sounds in a syllable are said together with no interruptions. It is almost as if the sounds are said as one sound. In English, a syllable has one vowel sound and may have several consonant sounds.

Some words have only one syllable:

one, where, you, thought

Some words have two syllables:

wait-ing, friend-ship, wor-ry

These are three syllable words:

ac-ci-dent, sim-i-lar, con-clu-sion

A. Listen to a pronunciation teacher introduce himself to the class. Pay special attention to the underlined words.

Hello everyone! Welcome to pronunciation class. My name is Jesse Granada, and I'll be your teacher this semester. We're going to learn about the rhythm, intonation, and sounds of English, and you'll all work on improving your comprehensibility. Now, open your books to page two. We're going to start by learning about syllables.

B. Listen to these words from the introduction and write down the number of syllables you hear. The first one is done for you.

1. __3__ everyone

2. _____ pronunciation

3. _____ semester

4. _____ rhythm

5. _____ sounds

6. _____ improving

7. _____ comprehensibility

8. _____ open

9. _____ page

10. _____ about

Listen again, and repeat each word after the speaker. Pay attention to the pronunciation of the syllables.

Some kinds of poetry require specific numbers of syllables in each line. Read these examples of haiku. Count the syllables on each line to learn the syllable rules for this kind of poetry.

Number of syllables per line

_____ Even these long days

_____ Are not nearly long enough

_____ For the birds to sing

—*Basho (1644–94)*

_____ I wish she were here

_____ To listen to me complain

_____ And enjoy this moon

—*issa (1763–1827)*

_____ A single leaf falls

_____ Then suddenly another

_____ Stolen by the wind

—*Ransetsu (1654–1707)*

Practice reading these poems out loud, pronouncing the syllables in each line of poetry.

Choose one of these topics and write your own haiku poem, using the correct number of syllables in each line. Then read your haiku to others in your class.

Common topics for haiku

- the beauty of nature
- description of a season of the year
- a feeling or emotion

_____

_____

_____

Chapter 2

Syllable Stress

In English, one syllable in each word is stressed more than the other syllables. A stressed syllable has a longer, louder, and higher sound than the other syllables in the word. The high points in the following pictures show the syllable stress for the words *student* and *computer*.

Examples:

STUD-ent

com-PU-ter

The rules for syllable stress in English are very complex. It is usually easiest to find the word stress of a new word by looking in a dictionary. If you would like to know more about the rules for syllable stress, see the *Sound Bites* website.

A. Listen to this conversation about registering for classes. Pay special attention to the underlined words.

A: Have you <u>registered</u> for <u>classes</u> for spring term yet?

B: No. I might do it <u>tomorrow</u>. Have you?

A: You <u>always</u> wait until the last <u>minute</u>. I registered on Tuesday.

B: It's <u>difficult</u> for me to make <u>decisions</u>. I can't decide if I want to take <u>geology</u> or geography. And I'm not sure if I want to take <u>photography</u> in the <u>morning</u> or the afternoon.

A: Decide soon, or there won't be any classes left!

B. Listen to these words from the conversation and underline the stressed syllable. The first one is done for you.

1. <u>re</u>gistered

2. classes

3. tomorrow

4. always

5. minute

6. difficult

7. decisions

8. geology

9. photography

10. morning

Listen again, and repeat each word after the speaker. Be sure to stress the correct syllable.

Some words can be either a noun or a verb. Nouns are usually stressed on the first syllable. Verbs are usually stressed on the second syllable.

Student A: Put an X next to **one** word in each of the following pairs. Do not tell Student B which word you marked. Read the word to your partner.

Student B: Listen to the word that your partner reads. In the following pairs, put an X next to the sentence that contains this word.

After you have completed all six items, compare your answers. Then switch roles and repeat the exercise.

1. _____ **RE**cord   _____ That athlete holds the world record in his sport.
   _____ re**CORD**   _____ Push this button and you can record your voice.

2. _____ **IN**sult   _____ That was a terrible insult.
   _____ in**SULT**   _____ He didn't mean to insult anyone.

3. _____ **PRE**sent   _____ She gave her mother an expensive present.
   _____ pre**SENT**   _____ Are you going to present in class today?

4. _____ **PRO**gress   _____ Use this chart to monitor your progress.
   _____ pro**GRESS**   _____ Work progressed very quickly.

5. _____ **PRO**ject   _____ This sounds like a fun project.
   _____ pro**JECT**   _____ Project the overhead while giving your speech.

6. _____ **OB**ject   _____ They found an interesting object.
   _____ ob**JECT**   _____ If you like the idea, I won't object.

Add at least one profession and one subject area to the lists below and mark the stressed syllables. Then discuss five of these professions with a partner or in a small group. What subjects should a person take to prepare for these professions? Be sure to pronounce the syllable stress for each profession and subject correctly.

Example: poliTICian

> **A:** If you want to be a politician, you should study geography.
>
> **B:** It's a good idea for a politician to know a foreign language, too.

Professions	Subjects
acCOUNtant	aNATomy
adminisTRAtive aSSIStant	biOLogy
aTTORney (LAWyer)	CHEMistry
BUSiness MANager	communiCAtions
comPUter PROgrammer	compoSItion
eCONomist	comPUter SCIence
opTICian	ecoNOMics
PHARmacist	eduCAtion
phySICian (DOCtor)	FOReign LANguage
TEAcher	geOGraphy
_____	HIStory
_____	matheMATics
	ALgebra
	geOMetry
	trigoNOMetry
	PHYsics
	_____
	_____

Chapter 3

Rhythm and Sentence Stress

In Chapter 2, you learned that English words have stressed and unstressed syllables. English *sentences* also have stressed and unstressed words. You should stress words that are used to express information — such as nouns, verbs, adjectives, adverbs, and question words. These are called *content words.** You should usually not stress words that are used mostly for grammatical purposes, such as articles, prepositions, conjunctions, helping verbs, and most pronouns. These are called *function words.*

When a content word has more than one syllable, the sentence stress falls on the word's stressed syllable. For more information on sentence stress and rhythm, see the *Sound Bites* website.

Think about the stress in the following words and phrases. Compare the stress in the word with the stress in the phrase, and notice the similarities between the two.

Example:	da	da	**DUM**	da
	con	cen	**TRA**	tion
	Can	you	**HELP**	us?
Example:	da	**DUM**	da	da
	im	**POSS**	i	ble
	They	**WANT**	ed	it.

*Words such as *this, that, these, those, yours, mine, ours, theirs, myself, yourself, himself, herself, yourselves, ourselves,* and *themselves* are also content words.

A. Limericks are poems that have a set number of stressed syllables in each line of the poem. Listen to this limerick, and write down the number of stressed syllables you hear in each line.

Number of stressed syllables per line

1. _____ There was a young lady of Niger

2. _____ Who smiled as she rode on a tiger.

3. _____ They returned from the ride

4. _____ With the lady inside

5. _____ And the smile on the face of the tiger.

    —*Anonymous*

B. Listen to this poem and pay attention to the rhythm of the stressed syllables. Notice there are three stressed syllables in each line of this poem, even though some lines have a total of three syllables, while others have six, seven, or nine total syllables. Listen again and snap your fingers or clap your hands on the stressed syllables. Do this several times until you feel comfortable with the rhythm.

Swing, swing, swing

A father and his child at the swings

Hands hold tight

She pretends that her feet are her wings

Strong arms push

"Higher" she giggles with glee

One, two, three

She's flying safe but free

Swing, swing, swing

—*April Lyndon*

Read the poem aloud. Be careful to pronounce the rhythm correctly.

Read these sentences along with the drumbeats on the tape. Be sure to pronounce the stressed syllables in time with the drumbeats. Try reading the sentences slowly at first, then read with the second set of drumbeats, which are at a faster pace.

THAT   CHILD   SINGS   SONGS.

THAT is   the CHILD   that SINGS   SONGS.

THAT is   the CHILD that is   SINGing   the SONGS.

THOSE are the CHILDren that are   SINGing   the SONGS.

THOSE are the CHILDren that have been SINGing   the SONGS.

THOSE are the CHILDren that have been SINGing all the SONGS.

   MOM   SAID   the BIKE   is MINE.

My MOM   SAID   the BIcycle   is MINE.

My MOM   TOLD me   the BIcycle   is MINE.

My MOM   TOLD me   the BIcycle will be MINE.

My MOTHer   has TOLD me   the BIcycle will be MINE.

My MOTHer has been TELLing me   the BIcycle will be MINE.

This poem has a very regular rhythm. There are two stressed syllables in the first two lines of each group, and there are three stressed syllables in the third line. Practice reading the poem with the correct rhythm. Work in three groups, with one group reading the role of the storyteller (A), the second group reading the kitten's role (B), and the third group reading the role of the mother cat (C). You can also practice reading in groups of three on your own.

A: Three little kittens,
They lost their mittens,
And they began to cry:

B: "Oh, mother, dear,
We sadly fear,
Our mittens we have lost."

C: "What! Lost your mittens?
You naughty* kittens!
Then you shall have no pie."

A: The three little kittens,
They found their mittens,
And they began to cry:

B: "Oh, mother, dear,
See here, see here!
Our mittens we have found."

C: "What! Found your mittens?
Then you're good kittens!
And you shall have some pie."

*Badly behaved

In English sentences, one word usually receives more stress on its stressed syllable than any other syllable in the sentence. Often this is the last content word in the sentence. However, changes in stress can be used to change the meaning of a sentence or to focus on important information. For example, the following common conversation would usually have this stress pattern:

A: Hi! How are you?

B: I'm fine. How are YOU?

A: I'm all right.

Notice that the second *you* gets extra stress. This is because speaker B wants to emphasize that the question now is directed at speaker A. That is, there is a change in the focus of the conversation from speaker B to speaker A. This extra stress, which shows a change in focus, is called *focal stress*.

Read these sentences for more examples of how focal stress can change the meaning of a sentence.

We watched a funny MOVie. (means: We watched a funny movie.)

We watched a FUNny movie. (means: It wasn't a scary or sad movie.)

WE watched a funny movie. (means: We did, but you didn't watch it.)

Focal stress is used to emphasize:

■ New information in a sentence

A: How was your vacation?

B: It was too SHORT.

■ Agreement or disagreement

A: Our vacation seemed short.

B: It WAS short.

■ A word or an idea that the speaker feels strongly about

A: Was your vacation short?

B: TOO short!

A. Listen to the conversation in the recording. The following question is repeated four times with different focal stress each time. Each time you hear the question, underline the word that receives focal stress.

1. _____ Why would Lou pay me back?

2. _____ Why would Lou pay me back?

3. _____ Why would Lou pay me back?

4. _____ Why would Lou pay me back?

B. Now, listen to the questions again. Match each question with the meaning created by the change in focal stress by writing the correct letter in the blank. Then practice saying the questions using all four focal stress patterns.

a. Lou owes someone money, but not me.

b. Lou never pays anyone back; he's too cheap.

c. I don't expect Lou to pay me back.

d. The money was a gift; there is no need to pay it back.

This is an excerpt from the play *Ashes to Ashes* by Harold Pinter. One way to use focal stress in each sentence has been marked with capital letters. With a partner, practice reading the lines, pronouncing the focal stress correctly. When you are ready, perform the dialog for your class.

Rebecca: I can't TELL you what he LOOKed like.

Devlin: Have you forGOTten?

Rebecca: No, I HAVEn't forgotten. But that's not the POINT. Anyway, he went away YEARS ago.

Devlin: Went aWAY? Where did he GO?

Rebecca: His JOB took him away. He had a JOB.

Devlin: What WAS it?

Rebecca: WHAT?

Devlin: What KIND of job was it? WHAT job?

Rebecca: I think it had something to do with a TRAVel agency. I think he was some kind of COURier. No. No, he WASn't. That was only a part-TIME job. I mean, that was only PART of the job in the agency. He was QUITE high up, you see. He had a lot of responsiBILities.

Pause

Devlin: What sort of AGency?

Rebecca: A TRAVel agency.

Devlin: What SORT of travel agency?

Rebecca: He was a GUIDE, you see. A GUIDE.

Devlin: A TOURist guide?

Pause

Rebecca: Did I ever tell you about that PLACE...about the time he took me to that PLACE?

Devlin: WHAT place?

Rebecca: I'm SURE I told you.

Devlin: No. You never TOLD me.

Rebecca: How FUNny. I could SWEAR I had. Told YOU.

Devlin: You haven't told me ANYthing. You've NEVer spoken about him before. You haven't told ME anything.

There may be more than one way to use focal stress in some of these lines. Try to say some of the lines with different focal stress patterns. How many different patterns can you find that make sense? How does changing the focal stress change the meaning of the sentence?

With a group of classmates, choose two or three of the sentences in this list. Take turns reading the sentence aloud, changing the emphasis on one piece of information. Remember to change the focal stress to emphasize the information that you changed. In your group, talk about how changing the stress changes the meaning. Try to see how many new sentences you can make.

Tom bought a new car last month.

We'll meet you at the restaurant at 7:00.

I have always wanted to visit Africa.

Linda's favorite food is strawberry pie.

Did you remember to call your mother?

Example:

A: STEVE was doing his homework when you called.

B: Steve was doing his HOMEwork when you called.

C: Steve was doing his homework when you CALLED.

D: Steve WAS doing his homework when you called.

E: Steve was doing his homework when YOU called.

You know that stressed syllables have longer, louder, and higher sounds than do unstressed syllables. When English speakers pronounce unstressed syllables quickly and quietly, the vowel sound in these syllables often changes to the sound /ə/. This sound is called a *schwa*, and is made by relaxing your tongue in the middle of your mouth. It sounds like "uh."*

In these words, the first syllable is unstressed and is pronounced with a schwa sound.

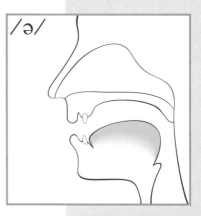

Examples: əBOUT   rəTURN   cənFUSE

In these words, the last syllable is unstressed and is pronounced with a schwa sound.

Examples: STRONGər   DATə   HELPfəl

The /ə/ sound occurs in most unstressed syllables. However, not all vowels are reduced. To learn about more exceptions, visit the *Sound Bites* website.

---

*In some dialects of American English, reduced vowels sound like /ɪ/. As long as you say unstressed vowels faster, softer, and at a lower pitch than you say stressed vowels, you may use either sound, and your English will be understandable.

Listen to these ten words and sentences. When you hear the word the first time, underline the stressed syllable. Then listen again and draw a line through the vowels that are reduced in the word. The first one is done for you.

1. stud<u>e</u>nt   I'm a student now.

2. become   I want to become a nurse.

3. classes   I've done well in my classes.

4. practical   Soon, I start my practical training.

5. hospital   I'll work at a hospital.

6. observe   There I can observe nurses at work

7. technical   I'll learn new technical skills too.

8. nervous   I guess I'll be nervous on the first day.

9. exciting   I think it will be exciting.

10. patients   I really want to help patients who need me.

Now, listen to the words and sentences again and repeat after the speaker. Practice the correct pronunciation of reduced vowels.

With a partner, think of at least two words that use each of the word parts in these lists. These word parts are almost always unstressed and should be pronounced with reduced vowel sounds. Share your words with others in your class, being careful to pronounce the words correctly.

com-/con-	dis-	ex-	in-
comPLAIN	disTURB	exPECT	inSTEAD
conVINCE	disCUSS	exAMine	inSPECT
_____	_____	_____	_____
_____	_____	_____	_____

-ful	-ion	-ical	-ness
HELPful	celeBRAtion	eLECtrical	HAPpiness
BEAUtiful	eduCAtion	PRACtical	USEfulness
_____	_____	_____	_____
_____	_____	_____	_____

For more information about how prefixes and suffixes affect syllable stress, see the *Sound Bites* website.

Focused Speaking Practice

Choose eight words from the lists on the previous page and write sentences using these words. Be sure you know which vowel sounds are reduced in each word. Read your sentences to a partner, a small group, or on a cassette recording.

When you study basic English grammar, you learn about contractions. Commonly contracted words include *not*, *will*, *would* and forms of the verbs *be* and *have*.

Examples:

I'm sure *that's* the right answer.

We *haven't* heard whether *they'll* be coming or not.

You've always got great ideas!

He's already gotten home.

I'd heard you were coming.

She'd like to help us.

Other words in English may also sound like they are contracted; this often happens with function words that are unstressed. Remember, though, that some function words should not be written as contractions, only pronounced to sound like contractions.

Examples:

does   When's* he usually call? (not written as a contraction)

did   What'd* they tell you? (not written as a contraction)

Any of these words can also be contracted with a noun, although such contractions are only spoken, and not written.

Examples:

are   My friends're* coming over tonight. (not written as a contraction)

had   Tammy'd* left before we got there. (not written as a contraction)

Contracting these words helps English speakers to stress content words and gives English its rhythm.

*For more information on the correct use of contractions, see the *Sound Bites* website.

A. Listen to the following sentences. Put an X in the correct column to show whether the speaker pronounces the long form or the contracted form. The first one is done for you.

	Long form	Contracted form
1. She has always done such nice things for people.		X
2. We had been looking for something like this.		
3. Where did you get that cool watch?		
4. You have done a terrific job.		
5. I hope you will show us how to do that.		
6. How does she do it?		
7. I have not ever seen anything I like more.		
8. I am very impressed with your work.		
9. We would love to see more of your photographs.		
10. Your shirt is fantastic.		
11. Your ideas are always so interesting.		
12. He has got great taste in clothes.		

B. Listen to this conversation about compliments, and write the long form of the contracted words. The first one is done for you.

A: You know, I think **(1)** _that_ _is_ a great color on you. **(2)** _____ _____ been wanting to tell you all day.

B: Why, thank you. **(3)** _____ _____ always been my favorite color. **(4)** _____ _____ glad you like it. **(5)** _____ _____ got great taste in clothes, so **(6)** _____ _____ a high compliment.

A: Well, **(7)** _____ _____ a nice thing to say!

B: You know, people **(8)** _____ _____ often say nice things like that anymore. **(9)** _____ _____ we stop complimenting each other?

A: I think **(10)** _____ _____ a little nervous that **(11)** _____ _____ think **(12)** _____ _____ being romantic.

B: **(13)** _____ _____ true. But I think **(14)** _____ _____ be nice if we all complimented each other more — as long as it **(15)** _____ _____ get too personal.

A: **(16)** _____ _____ remember that you like a compliment now and then.

B: Speaking of compliments, your presentation last week was terrific. **(17)** _____ _____ you work with on the project?

A: LeeAnn. **(18)** _____ _____ been doing great work lately. **(19)** _____ _____ hoped **(20)** _____ _____ notice.

Now read the conversation with a partner, and pronounce the words you have written as contractions.

This is an excerpt from the play *The Time of Your Life* by William Saroyan. Saroyan has used contractions to make the lines the actors say sound like natural English speech. With a partner, practice reading the lines, pronouncing the contractions correctly. When you are ready, perform the dialog for your class.

Kitty: Where is Tom?

Joe: He's getting a job tonight driving a truck. He'll be back in a couple of days.

Kitty: I said I'd marry him.

Joe: He wanted to see you and say good-by.

Kitty: He's too good for me. He's like a little boy. I'm — Too many things have happened to me.

Joe: Kitty Duval, you're one of the few truly innocent people I have ever known. He'll be back in a couple of days. Go back to the hotel and wait for him.

Kitty: That's what I mean. I can't stand being alone. I'm no good. I tried very hard. I don't know what it is. I miss —

Joe: Do you really want to come back here, Kitty?

Kitty: I don't know. I'm not sure. Everything smells different. I don't know how to feel, or what to think. I know I don't belong there. It's what I've wanted all my life, but it's too late. I try to be happy about it, but all I can do is remember everything and cry.

Joe: I don't know what to tell you, Kitty. I didn't mean to hurt you.

Kitty: You haven't hurt me. You're the only person who's ever been good to me. I've never known anybody like you. I'm not sure about love any more, but I know I love you, and I know I love Tom.

With a partner, choose one of the following situations. Write a conversation between two people in the situation. Use contractions whenever possible — even those that do not usually appear in written English. Practice your conversation and then perform it for others in your class.

- A person compliments a co-worker on a project that was very well done.

- Neighbors meet on the street. One neighbor shows the other his or her newborn daughter for the first time. The neighbors talk about the baby.

- Two people are having dinner together. One person cooked the meal, and the second person compliments the other on the delicious food.

- Two friends are looking at the brand new car that one of them just bought and talking about all of the nice features of the car.

_____

_____

_____

_____

_____

_____

_____

_____

_____

_____

_____

_____

_____

_____

_____

_____

Words are only one way to give a listener information. Intonation also expresses meaning when you speak. Intonation is the way your voice rises and falls when you speak, and it can tell a listener many things. It can tell a listener if you are sure that what you are saying is true, or it can let a listener know that you are not finished speaking. Intonation can also be used to express interest, sarcasm, and anger — along with many other emotions and attitudes.

Tip

If intonation is difficult for you to hear, you will have to train your ear to listen to how the voice rises and falls. If you have trouble hearing intonation, try covering your ears with your hands while you listen so that you cannot hear the speaker's words. You will be able to hear just the intonation! Of course, you should only do this when practicing pronunciation, and not in conversations with your friends!

Chapter 7

Thought Groups and Pausing

Sentences are the basic units of written language. However, if you listen closely when people speak English, you might notice that they don't always speak in complete sentences. In fact, when we talk, we use a different basic unit than the sentence. In this book, we call this basic unit a *thought group*. A thought group may be a sentence or a phrase, but it always:

- Has a short pause before and after the thought group (sometimes very short!)

- Has an *intonation curve*, a pattern of pitch change that either rises or falls at the end of the thought group

- Has one word that receives focal stress

It is also important to remember that a thought group always keeps grammatical units together. If you pause between grammatical units that should stay together, you will not sound fluent.

Here is an example of three thought groups that sound fluent:

Tomorrow, / if the weather is nice, / let's go to the park.

Here is an example of three thought groups that do not sound fluent:

Tomorrow if / the weather is nice, let's / go to the park.

Notice that in written English, commas and periods often show where thought groups can end. However, not all speakers divide thought groups in exactly the same way.

A. Listen to how two speakers use thought groups differently. Listen for pauses, intonation, and logical ideas, and draw a line at the end of each thought group you hear. The first one is done for you.

1. Why does the weather affect my life more than my life affects the weather?*

2. Why does the weather affect my life more than my life affects the weather?

3. If you don't like the weather, just wait and it will change.

4. If you don't like the weather, just wait and it will change.

B. The punctuation has been left out of this weather report, so you must listen to hear where the thought groups end. Draw a line between each thought group. The first two have been done for you.

You'll like today's weather report / it's going to be a beautiful day / the skies are mostly sunny there will be a few clouds but just in the afternoon the high will be 72 degrees the low 65 tonight will be partly cloudy and a little chilly the low will be 52 degrees so take a sweater if you'll be outside enjoy the warm sunny weather while it lasts next weekend we're expecting it to be cold and rainy.

Now read the weather report aloud, and pause where you have marked the ends of thought groups.

—Ashleigh Brilliant

Guided Pronunciation Practice

Working with a partner, think of a way to end each sentence below, but do not write your answers. Then read the sentence and your ending to your partner. Try to speak fluently, pausing only at the end of thought groups.

1. Last Thursday...
2. Are those books...?
3. My favorite place...
4. Before we get started...
5. While I was watching TV...
6. Even though you came early...
7. What did you do...?
8. As soon as the phone rang...
9. First, I want...
10. Did he tell...?

Work with a group of classmates to create a story. Each person in your group must add one thought group to the story. Use the picture below for ideas, or create your own story. Be careful to pause only at the ends of thought groups as you tell the story.

Intonation is the rise and fall of your voice when you speak. Every thought group has an intonation curve. The intonation rises or falls around the word in the thought group that receives focal stress. (For more information about focal stress, see Chapter 4.)

Basic Intonation Pattern 1: Sure and Unsure. Intonation can show whether you are sure or unsure about what you are saying.

- Rising intonation can show that you are unsure about what you are saying.

- Falling intonation makes you sound sure and confident. (See Chapter 9 to learn about the exception for *Wh* questions.)

Example:

Sure   She likes spicy food.

Unsure   She likes spicy food?*

Punctuation: In informal writing, you can use a question mark to show rising intonation when something is unsure.

Basic Intonation Pattern 2: Finished and Unfinished. Intonation can show if you have completed an idea, or if you plan to continue.

- Use a slight rise in intonation when you are pausing between thought groups, but plan to continue speaking.

- Use a sharp fall in intonation at the end of a complete statement. You may continue to speak after using falling intonation, but the fall lets the listener know that the idea is complete.

Example:

Finished speaking   My favorite food is sushi.

Will continue speaking   I like rice and beans, but... (I don't want them for dinner tonight.)

Punctuation: Three periods (...) can show that a speaker is not finished talking.

*In informal speech, people sometimes make questions out of statements by using rising intonation.

Intonation Pattern 1: Sure and Unsure

Listen to this conversation between a restaurant server and a diner. Pay attention to the intonation in each thought group, and mark whether the speaker sounds sure or unsure. The first one is done for you.

Listening
Practice

Server: My name is Renata.	1. (Sure)	Unsure
I'll be your server today.	2. Sure	Unsure
Ready to order?	3. Sure	Unsure
Diner: I guess so.	4. Sure	Unsure
Server: Need a few more minutes?	5. Sure	Unsure
Diner: Yeah. I need a few more minutes.	6. Sure	Unsure

Intonation Pattern 2: Finished and Unfinished

Listen to this conversation between a restaurant server and a diner. Pay attention to the intonation of the thought groups, and mark whether the statement sounds finished or unfinished.

Server: It looks like you're ready now.	7. Finished Unfinished
Diner: Yes. I'd like a tossed salad	8. Finished Unfinished
and the spaghetti.	9. Finished Unfinished
Server: OK. One spaghetti,	10. Finished Unfinished
one salad...	11. Finished Unfinished
...and some dressing for the salad.	12. Finished Unfinished
Italian, ranch, blue cheese...	13. Finished Unfinished
Diner: Ranch sounds good.	14. Finished Unfinished
Put it on the side, please.	15. Finished Unfinished
Server: I'll bring it right out.	16. Finished Unfinished

Each of the following groups of dialogs contains the same thought groups, but in different orders. The intonation is different in each dialog. Use the punctuation to help you determine the correct intonation for each dialog. Read the dialogs below with a partner. Be careful to pronounce the intonation correctly.

Dialog Group 1

A: He's coming.

B: At 8:00?

A: After work.

B: Really?

A: He called.

A: He called?

B: At 8:00.

A: He's coming?

B: After work.

A: Really?

A: He called at 8:00, …

B: Really?

A: He's coming after work.

B: Really?

A: Really!

Dialog Group 2

A: Today was a long day?

B: Very.

A: You're tired?

B: Yes.

A: You want some tea…

B: Maybe later.

A: Or coffee?

B: Not yet.

A: You want some tea or coffee?

B: Not yet.

A: Maybe later?

B: Maybe later.

A: You're tired?

B: Today was a long day.

A: Very?

B: Yes.

A: Today was a long day.

B: Very?

A: Yes.

B: You're tired. You want some tea or coffee?

A: Not yet… Maybe later.

Chapter 8   37

Focused Speaking Practice

To practice these two intonation concepts, write a short dialog about someone who is in a hurry and is trying to order a meal in a restaurant where the cook and the wait staff are very slow. After you write your dialog, mark the intonation and perform it with a partner.

_____

_____

_____

_____

_____

_____

_____

_____

_____

_____

_____

_____

_____

Rising and falling intonation can have many different meanings, but it's used most commonly to indicate questions and statements.

- In an ordinary English statement, use falling intonation on the last content word in the thought group.

Examples:

I'm going to the store.

She wants to speak to him.

- In a yes/no question, use rising intonation — usually on the last content word in the question.

Examples:

Are you going to the store?

Does she want to speak to him?

- Information questions have a special intonation pattern. These questions start with the question words *who*, *what*, *when*, *where*, *why*, *which*, and *how*. On the last content word in the question, use rising intonation and then finish the sentence with falling intonation.

Examples:

Where are you going?

Who does she want to talk to?

Note: In informal speech, people sometimes make questions out of statements by using rising intonation.

Example:

You're going to the store again? You were just there yesterday!

Listen to a conversation between a renter and an apartment manager. Match each thought group with the intonation curve showing the kind of intonation you hear. The first one is done for you.

Intonation Curves

a. _____

b. _____

c. _____

1. __*b*__ **Renter:** Do you have any apartments for rent?

2. _____ **Manager:** Is a one-bedroom apartment OK?

3. _____ I have a one-bedroom for rent.

4. _____ **Renter:** What's the monthly rent?

5. _____ **Manager:** It's nine hundred dollars a month.

6. _____ **Renter:** Which utilities are included?

7. _____ **Manager:** Water, trash, electricity, and gas are included.

8. _____ You pay your own telephone and cable TV.

9. _____ **Renter:** How are the neighbors here?

10. _____ Are they nice?

11. _____ **Manager:** The neighbors are great.

12. _____ I think you would like them!

Listen to the dialog again, and repeat after the speakers. Then perform the dialog with a partner, making sure to pronounce the intonation correctly.

Student A: Put an X next to **one** phrase in each of the pairs in the left-hand column. Do not tell Student B which phrase you marked. Then read the phrase to Student B using the correct intonation.

Student B: Listen to the phrase that Student A reads, and put an X next to the correct ending from the right-hand column.

After you and your partner have completed all six items, compare your answers. Then reverse roles and repeat the exercise.

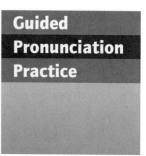

1. _____ "This apartment has two bedrooms?"   _____ "Yes, it does."

   _____ This apartment has two bedrooms,   _____ and the one next door has three.

2. _____ "There's a laundry room downstairs?"   _____ "Yes. Every tenant has a key."

   _____ There's a laundry room downstairs,   _____ but it's always really busy.

3. _____ "You have a roommate?"   _____ "No. My friend is staying here."

   _____ You have a roommate.   _____ Her name is Irene, right?

4. _____ "Rent is due on the first of the month?"   _____ "Yes — or you must pay a late fee."

   _____ Rent is due on the first of the month,   _____ but I get paid on the second.

5. _____ "The apartment is furnished?"   _____ "No. Those across the street are."

   _____ The apartment is furnished,   _____ but I don't like the furniture.

Read this advertisement about an apartment for rent. Add three or more questions to the list below. Then, with a partner, role-play a conversation between the renter and the landlord. Switch roles so that you both get to practice both questions AND answers.

FOR RENT 2 bedroom apartment with a great view! pool, parking, laundry clean and quiet—no pets

Questions to ask the landlord:

Are utilities included?

Where is the laundry room?

Is the stove gas or electric?

How long is the lease?

_____

_____

_____

_____

_____

_____

Tag questions are short questions that follow statements. The intonation used on the short question, or *tag*, can change the meaning.

Pattern 1: Speaker is Sure of the Answer. When you are sure of the answer and expect your listener to agree, use falling intonation on the tag.

Example:

Pattern 2: Speaker is Unsure of the Answer. When you are unsure of the answer and expect the listener to answer the question, use rising intonation on the tag.

Example:

For information on the grammatical formation of tag questions, see the *Sound Bites* website.

Listen to this dialog between a mother and her child. The first time you listen, fill in the tag for each tag question that you hear. Then listen again and circle the word *sure* if the speaker uses rising intonation or *unsure* if the speaker uses falling intonation. The first one is done for you.

Child: Mommy? There really is a

Santa Claus, ___*isn't there*___ ?   1. Sure ⃝Unsure

Mother: You believe in him, _____?   2. Sure   Unsure

Child: Uh huh.

Mother: Well, if you believe in him, he's real,

_____?   3. Sure   Unsure

Child: Then, I guess I should believe in him,

_____?   4. Sure   Unsure

Mother: He brings you presents every year,

_____?   5. Sure   Unsure

Child: Yes. He'll bring them this year too,

_____?   6. Sure   Unsure

Mother: You sent him a list, _____?   7. Sure   Unsure

And, you haven't been bad

this year, _____?   8. Sure   Unsure

Child: I don't think I have, _____?   9. Sure   Unsure

Mother: Of course not. Now, you shouldn't be

awake this late, _____?   10. Sure   Unsure

Child: Mommy, you know everything,

_____?   11. Sure   Unsure

Now read the dialog with a partner. Be sure to pronounce the intonation as the speakers in the recording do.

Read each of the following dialogs. Decide whether the intonation should rise or fall on the tag questions, then practice reading the dialogs with a partner. Be sure to use the correct intonation.

Dialog 1

A: Is there anything good on TV tonight?

B: It's Thursday!

A: Oh, yeah! "The Doctors" is on tonight, isn't it?

B: It sure is. Every Thursday at 8 p.m.

Dialog 2

A: Hello?

B: Hi. It's me. I'm still at the airport.

A: Oh no. Your flight wasn't delayed again, was it?

B: Yeah. The weather is terrible.

Dialog 3

A: Janet is going to the concert tomorrow, isn't she?

B: I don't know. She didn't say.

A: I'll call and ask her if she is. I need a ride.

Dialog 4

A: I'm going out for awhile.

B: You'll be back before dinner, won't you?

A: Yeah, why?

B: You promised to help me with my homework.

Focused Speaking Practice

How well do you know your classmates? First, read each of the tag questions below, and add two questions of your own. Then, for each question, write down the name of a classmate to whom you will ask this question. Mark whether you are sure or unsure how your classmates will answer. Then use the correct intonation to ask your classmates the questions.

Name of classmate you will ask	Tag question	Sure ↘	Unsure ↗
_____	1. You play a musical instrument, don't you?	_____	_____
_____	2. You went to the movies last month, didn't you?	_____	_____
_____	3. You have flown on an airplane, haven't you?	_____	_____
_____	4. You were good at math in school, weren't you?	_____	_____
_____	5. You won't be working this weekend, will you?	_____	_____
_____	6. You don't have a roommate, do you?	_____	_____
_____	7. You weren't absent last week, were you?	_____	_____
_____	8. You aren't coming to school on Saturday, are you?	_____	_____
_____	_____	_____	_____
_____	_____	_____	_____

Two different intonation patterns are used when an English speaker wants to offer a listener a choice. One pattern is used when there are only two options, and the other is used when the two examples you are giving are not the only options.

Pattern 1: Closed Choice. When you are suggesting only two choices, use rising intonation on the first item and falling intonation on the second item. Falling intonation is used because the list of choices is finished.

Example:

A: For the holidays, do you want to visit your parents or my parents?

B: We spent the holiday with your parents last year. Let's visit mine.

Pattern 2: Open Choice. When you are making suggestions, but you know that there might be other options, use rising intonation on both items.

Example:

A: What kind of restaurant do you want to go to? Chinese? Mexican?

B: How about Italian? We haven't had Italian food in awhile.

As a listener, understanding these patterns can help you to be more polite when a speaker offers you a choice, because you will know whether the speaker expects you to choose only from the items listed, or whether it is OK to make additional suggestions.

Listen to this dialog about two friends making vacation plans. Then listen to six questions from the dialog. Mark whether each question has a closed choice or an open choice intonation pattern. The first one is done for you.

	Closed choice ↗↘	Open choice ↗↗
1. We could go to the beach... visit New York City...		X
2. Do you want to go to Joshua Tree or Arches National Park?	___	___
3. So, do you like to camp in a tent or stay at a lodge?	___	___
4. We could take my car or your truck. Which is better?	___	___
5. Should we plan to stay for three days? Four?	___	___
6. I'll start gathering information about the park, like maps... guidebooks....	___	___

Listen to these six questions again, and repeat after the speaker. Be sure to use the same intonation pattern that the speaker uses.

Student A: Put an X next to **one** question in each of the pairs in the left-hand column. Do not tell Student B which item you marked. Read the question to Student B using the correct intonation.

Student B: Listen to the question that Student A reads, and put an X next to the correct response in the right-hand column.

After you and your partner have completed all four items, compare your answers. Then reverse roles and repeat the exercise.

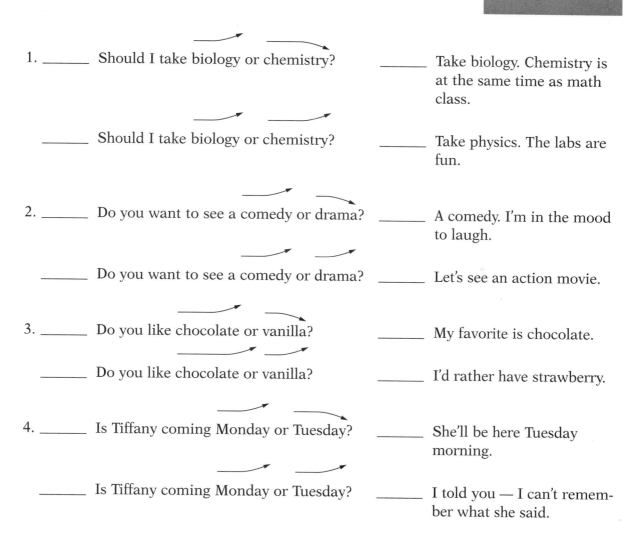

1. _____ Should I take biology or chemistry? _____ Take biology. Chemistry is at the same time as math class.

_____ Should I take biology or chemistry? _____ Take physics. The labs are fun.

2. _____ Do you want to see a comedy or drama? _____ A comedy. I'm in the mood to laugh.

_____ Do you want to see a comedy or drama? _____ Let's see an action movie.

3. _____ Do you like chocolate or vanilla? _____ My favorite is chocolate.

_____ Do you like chocolate or vanilla? _____ I'd rather have strawberry.

4. _____ Is Tiffany coming Monday or Tuesday? _____ She'll be here Tuesday morning.

_____ Is Tiffany coming Monday or Tuesday? _____ I told you — I can't remember what she said.

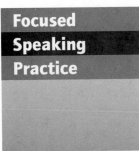
You and your partner have decided to cook dinner for some friends. Think of at least two more choices for each course on the menu and write them in the chart below. Discuss the choices with your partner, making sure to use the correct intonation. Write your completed menu in the space provided in the second chart.

Choices for Dinner Menu

Appetizer	Chips & salsa	_____	_____	_____
Soup or salad	Pea soup	_____	_____	_____
Main dish	Salmon	_____	_____	_____
Side dish	Carrots	_____	_____	_____
Dessert	Ice cream	_____	_____	_____
Beverage	Lemonade	_____	_____	_____

Dinner Menu

Appetizer	_____
Soup or salad	_____
Main dish	_____
Side dish	_____
Dessert	_____
Beverage	_____

When you list two or more points or ideas, intonation lets the listener know when the list begins and when it ends.

Pattern 1: Complete List. When you are listing things, the intonation rises for each point except the last one. On the last point, the intonation falls; this means that the list is complete.

Example:

A: What countries have you visited?

B: Just three. India, Malaysia, and Germany.

Pattern 2: Incomplete List. If you want the list to continue, such as when you are just giving a few examples, use rising intonation on all items to show that the list is incomplete.

Example:

A: What countries have you visited?

B: India, Malaysia, Germany... I've been to so many, it's hard to remember them all.

First, read the following six sentences from a lecture on digital information. Then listen to the lecture. After you hear the lecture you will hear these six sentences. Pay attention to the intonation and mark whether each underlined list is complete, or whether it is an incomplete list of examples. The first one is done for you.

1. Digital information can be stored—on disks, on DVDs, on the backs of credit cards.

    1. Complete (Incomplete)

2. Information is a collection of facts or data.

    2. Complete   Incomplete

3. Those facts or data can take many forms: a novel, a photograph, a simple yes or no.

    3. Complete   Incomplete

4. The only numbers a computer understands are zero and one.

    4. Complete   Incomplete

5. Computer software, working together with hardware, can store, retrieve, process, compress, or encrypt this digital information.

    5. Complete   Incomplete

6. Digital information can also be sent over phone wires, by satellites, over wireless networks.

    6. Complete   Incomplete

Now listen to the six sentences from the lecture again, and repeat after the speaker, being sure to use the same intonation patterns.

Choose three of the categories listed below, and write down three items that fit into each category you chose. Tell your partner the three items in the category, but do not name the category. Use intonation that rises on every item in the list except the last one. Your partner will guess the name of the category into which these three items fit.

Example:

    A: This category includes cows, cats, and canaries.

    B: Is it animals that begin with the letter C?

Animals that begin with C	**Types of transportation**	**Things you do in the morning**
Cows	_____	_____
Cats	_____	_____
Canaries	_____	_____

Furniture	**Countries in South America**	**Famous singers**
_____	_____	_____
_____	_____	_____
_____	_____	_____

Vegetables	**Clothing that begins with S**	**Things you eat for breakfast**
_____	_____	_____
_____	_____	_____
_____	_____	_____

Variation: Play the same game, but use rising intonation for all three items in the list. This means that your list is unfinished. Your partner should try to add a fourth item that fits into the category.

Example:

    A: This category includes eggs, cereal, toast...

    B: and oatmeal. It's things you eat for breakfast, right?

To practice intonation for lists, play the shopping game. Sit in a circle with a group of classmates. The person who starts says:

"I went shopping and I bought _____."

and finishes the sentence with a kind of food, such as "I went shopping, and I bought apple juice."

Each person adds an item to the list, first naming all of the foods mentioned before in the correct order. You can also play this game by naming foods for each letter of the alphabet. Remember to use rising intonation on every item on the list except for the very last item.

Example:

A: I went to the store, and I bought apple juice.

B: I went to the store, and I bought apple juice and baby food.

C: I went to the store, and I bought apple juice, baby food, and canned corn.

D: I went to the store, and I bought apple juice, baby food, canned corn, and doughnuts.

Hint: Move your hand up as you say each item in the list except for the last item. On the last item, move your hand down. This will remind you to use the correct intonation.

People often show emotions and attitudes using body language and facial expression. However, without seeing someone, such as during a telephone conversation, you can still tell how people feel by listening to their voice and intonation. These cues, along with changes in focal stress, will help you understand and send spoken messages that say more than words alone can. (See Chapter 4 for more information about focal stress.)

Neutral, everyday intonation shows little emotion. This is the basic statement intonation pattern described in Chapter 9. These statements are usually spoken at normal speed and loudness.

That was a good answer.

(What a good student.)

Enthusiastic or happy intonation rises and falls sharply. The speaker may also speak more quickly and loudly.

That was a good answer!

(I'm very proud of you!)

Angry intonation also has sharp changes in intonation, but usually the intonation starts much lower. Words are spoken quickly with strong emphasis.

That was a good answer!

(I should have gotten an A not a D!)

Sarcastic intonation is flat and low. The syllable receiving focal stress may be very long and slow, and focal stress usually comes early in the thought group, rather than at the end. Sarcastic intonation means the exact opposite of the words that are spoken.

THAT was a good answer.

(That is the stupidest answer I've ever heard.)

You will hear this short dialog four times. Each time, the intonation conveys a different emotion. Number each emotion in the order that you hear it. The first one is done for you.

A: Look.

B: What?

A: This.

B: That?

A: Yeah.

B: Wow.

A: Interesting?

B: Sure.

Emotions

_____ Neutral, everyday intonation

__1__ Excitement and happiness

_____ Anger

_____ Sarcasm

What might be the context for each of these conversations? Listen again, and discuss a situation in which two speakers might use each intonation pattern. Then practice reading the dialog with a partner. Try to convey each of these emotions.

Work with a partner. From the box, choose an emotion or attitude for each speaker in these dialogs. Read the dialog with your partner and use intonation to convey this emotion or attitude. Your classmates will listen to your dialog and guess the emotion or attitude you are conveying.

Guided Pronunciation Practice

Dialog 1

A: How do you think you did on the test?

B: I guess I did OK. I had trouble with part two.

A: Me too. I thought it was hard.

B: Well, we'll find out on Friday.

Dialog 2

A: What are you watching?

B: Some TV show.

A: Oh, I know this show. I think it is funny.

B: Really? I think it is pretty stupid.

A: Then why don't you change the channel?

B: All the other shows are even dumber.

Dialog 3

A: What's the weather like outside?

B: I guess it's pretty nice.

A: Don't you know?

B: I haven't been outside yet today.

Emotions and Attitudes

Happiness
Sarcasm
Anger

With a partner, choose one of the following situations. Write a dialog about this situation, and use various intonation patterns to convey different emotions in your dialog.

Situations

- You meet for the first time at a party. You discover that you like the same kind of music, and you dislike the same movies.

- You are on a TV talk show together. You have been asked to talk about a topic (political, ethical, or other) about which you disagree strongly.

- You are shopping together and looking at the clothes on the sales rack. You make sarcastic jokes about the ugly clothing that you see. You also find some good bargains.

- You work together and your boss has given you too little time to finish a project. She says it is urgent. You are discussing the schedule to figure out how you will meet your deadlines.

- It is Friday night and you are both bored. You are trying to figure out what to do. No matter what suggestions one of you makes, the other does not find them interesting.

- You and your partner are fans of different sports teams. These teams will play against each other this weekend. You are discussing who will win.

English has many vowel sounds. Most languages have five or six vowel sounds, but English has fifteen!* Different vowel sounds are made when you change the shape inside your mouth by moving your tongue and your lips. If this sounds confusing, think about what happens when you blow across the top of a bottle. You get a different sound when the bottle is empty than you do when it has some water in it. The same is true of the sounds you make with your mouth, only instead of water, you use your tongue and lips to change the sound. The charts on the next page show the placement of the tongue for all of the vowel sounds of English. You will probably not need to practice every chapter in Part Three. Choose the chapters that focus on the vowel sounds that are difficult for you. If you aren't sure which vowel sounds give you trouble, do the diagnostic test on the *Sound Bites* website.

*Some dialects of English have more or fewer vowels sounds than this, but fifteen is about standard.

Tip

The pronunciation of individual vowel sounds varies slightly from one speaker to another. However, every native speaker of English can make and hear the differences among all of the sounds. It is most important that each vowel sound be different from the sounds that are most similar to it. For this reason, it is good to practice vowel sounds together — to train your ear to hear the differences, and to train your mouth to make the vowels sound different.

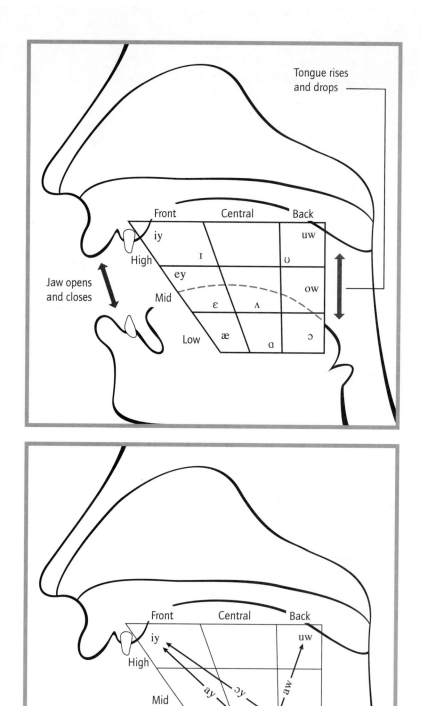

Chapter 14

Vowels that End in /y/ and /w/ Glides

Some vowel sounds in English require you to move your tongue as you say them. These vowels are often called *long vowels*. It does take slightly longer to say these vowels because at the end of the vowel, your tongue moves, or glides, toward a /y/ or a /w/ sound.* In this book, the symbols for these vowels include the /y/ and /w/ to help you remember how to pronounce them. These four vowel sounds are:

/iy/   as in m**ea**n

/ey/   as in m**ai**n

/uw/   as in m**oo**n

/ow/   as in m**oa**n

These sounds are often confused with similar short vowel sounds in which the tongue doesn't move at all. Compare the first vowel, which ends in /y/, with the second, shorter vowel, which does not end in /y/.

/iy/	as in t**ea**m	/ɪ/	as in T**i**m
/ey/	as in l**a**te	/ɛ/	as in l**e**t

In these examples, compare the first vowel, which ends in /w/, with the second, shorter vowel, which does not end in /w/.

/uw/	as in f**oo**l	/ʊ/	as in f**u**ll
/ow/	as in wr**o**te	/ɑ/	as in r**o**t

*In Chapter 15, you will learn about diphthongs. To make these sounds, your tongue will move even more than it does for these long vowels.

A. Listen and circle the word you hear. Then, mark whether the vowel sound in that word has a /y/ or /w/ glide, or if the vowel sound has no glide. The first one is done for you.

/iy/	or	/ɪ/	/y/ glide	No /y/ glide
1. (least)		list	✗	
2. wheel		will		
3. heat		hit		

/ey/	or	/ɛ/	/y/ glide	No /y/ glide
4. wait		wet		
5. pain		pen		
6. gate		get		

/uw/	or	/ʊ/	/w/ glide	No /w/ glide
7. boot		but		
8. pool		pull		
9. Luke		look		

/ow/	or	/ɑ/	/w/ glide	No /w/ glide
10. note		not		
11. robe		rob		
12. hope		hop		

B. The /y/ and /w/ sounds at the end of these vowels are especially noticeable when a word ending in one of these vowel sounds is followed by a word beginning with a vowel. Listen to these sentences and pay attention to the underlined words. Write a *y* or *w* above the words to show which of the two sounds you hear. The first one is done for you.

1. I won't <u>pay *y* another</u> penny.

2. Did you <u>see anyone</u> standing there?

3. I didn't <u>know about</u> the accident.

4. <u>Who is</u> going to call us?

5. It's on at <u>two o'clock</u>.

6. Don't <u>go out</u> without your umbrella.

7. He didn't tell <u>me anything</u>.

8. <u>May I</u> help you?

Now listen again and repeat the sentences after the speaker. Pay attention to the pronunciation of the vowels that end in /y/ or /w/.

Guided Pronunciation Practice
Student A

Student A: You will work with this page. Student B will work with page 66. For each box below, circle either of the two words or phrases. Dictate these sentences to Student B, who will write down the words you say in the blanks on page 66. Then reverse roles. The phrases in the Word Box will help you with spelling.

Word Box

Jean
Jane
vacuums
every two months

Three Roommates

[Joan / June] is the [neatest / cleanest]. She [changes the sheets / straightens up] nearly every [week / day].

[Joan / June] is [usually / routinely] helpful too.

She cleaned the __________ just last __________.

However, __________ is very lazy. She __________ the __________ only ____________________.

With a group of your classmates, discuss each of these actions, and think of three reasons why a person might do each one. The underlined words have vowels with glides. Be careful to pronounce them correctly.

Example:

>Why might you sl**ee**p during the d**ay**?
>
>I might sleep during the day if…
>
>>I were really tired.*
>>
>>I had to work at night.
>>
>>I planned to go out later.

1. Why might you **ea**t no f**oo**d for a wh**o**le d**ay**?

2. Why might you p**ai**nt your f**a**ce blue?

3. Why might you g**o** to sch**oo**l with b**a**re f**ee**t?

4. Why might you r**ea**d a n**ew** book **ea**ch w**ee**k?

5. Why might you not sh**ow** up for a d**a**te?

6. Why might you cl**o**se the door and st**ay** al**o**ne in your r**oo**m?

*These sentences are hypothetical conditionals. When the pronoun *I* is the subject in a hypothetical conditional sentence, the correct form of the verb BE is *were*. A grammar book can give you more information about this grammar structure.

Student B: You will work with this page. Student A will work with page 64. Listen to Student A, and in the blanks below, write down the words Student A says. Next, for each box, circle either of the two words or phrases. Dictate these sentences to Student A, who will write down the words you say in the blanks on page 64. The phrases in the Word Box will help you with spelling.

Three Roommates

_____ is the _____. She _____

nearly every _____.

_____ is _____ helpful too.

She cleaned the [stove / home] just last [week / Tuesday].

However, [Jean / Jane] is very lazy. She [sweeps / vacuums] the

[room / place] only [yearly / every two months].

Word Box

Joan
June
changes the
    sheets
straightens up
routinely

The three English vowel sounds that you will practice in this chapter are actually combinations of two sounds. They are called *diphthongs*. For the diphthongs /ay/, /aw/, and /ɔy/, you start by pronouncing the first sound, and then move your tongue and lips to make the second sound.

/ay/

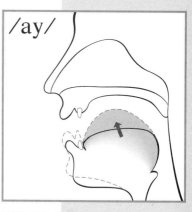

Start with /ɑ/ and move to /y/.
The lips move from open and rounded to slightly closed and spread.
The tongue moves from low in the center of the mouth to high in the front of the mouth.
The jaw rises.

Listen to examples of words with the /ay/ sound: fl**y**, s**i**gn, r**i**ght

/aw/

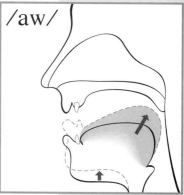

Start with /ɑ/ and move to /w/.
The lips move from open and rounded to slightly closed and rounded.
The tongue moves from low in the center of the mouth to high in the back of the mouth.
The jaw rises.

Listen to examples of words with the /aw/ sound: n**ow**, br**ow**n, sh**ou**t

/ɔy/

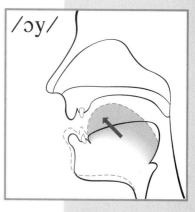

Start with /ɔ/ and move to /y/.
The lips move from closed and rounded to slightly closed and spread.
The tongue moves from low in the back of the mouth to high in the front of the mouth.
The jaw rises.

Listen to examples of words with the /ɔy/ sound: b**oy**, c**oi**n, m**oi**st

A. Listen to the telephone conversation between two friends who are planning a weekend together. Write in the missing words as you hear them. The first one is done for you.

A: I'm excited about coming to visit this weekend. What are we going to do?

B: There's a restaurant I've **(1)** ___found___ that I think you'll **(2)** _____. So we'll go there. And I want to go up into the **(3)** _____ to look at the **(4)** _____. The stars are really **(5)** _____ there at night.

A: It **(6)** _____ beautiful. But you know I don't really like **(7)** _____. How far up are we going to go?

B: It's not very **(8)** _____. And it's really worth it. The next day you have a **(9)** _____. We can either **(10)** _____ my friends at a concert, or if you want to **(11)** _____ the **(12)** _____ and **(13)** _____, we can stay home and watch a movie.

A: It doesn't matter to me. We can flip a **(14)** _____.

B: I can't wait to show you **(15)** _____.

B. Listen to the pronunciation of these words. Place each word in the column for the vowel sound it contains. The first one is done for you.

/ɔy/ as in coin	/ay/ as in fly	/aw/ as in brown
1. _____	_____	_found_
2. _____	_____	_____
3. _____	_____	_____
4. _____	_____	_____
5. _____	_____	_____
6. _____	_____	_____
7. _____	_____	_____
8. _____	_____	_____
9. _____	_____	_____
10. _____	_____	_____
11. _____	_____	_____
12. _____	_____	_____
13. _____	_____	_____
14. _____	_____	_____
15. _____	_____	_____

Now listen to these words again and repeat after the speaker. Be careful to pronounce the diphthongs correctly.

Guided Pronunciation Practice
Student A

Student A: Look at the chart below. Student B will work with the chart on page 72. Ask your partner questions to find out the hobbies that are missing for the people on your chart. Your partner will ask you similar questions to find out the hobbies that are missing from the chart on page 72.

Example:

Student A: What does Ms. Moyer do?

Student B: Ms. Moyer takes voice lessons. How about Ms. Boyd? What does she do?

/ɔy/	Ms. Moyer	Ms. Boyd	Roy	Mrs. Doyle
	takes voice lessons.	______________.	collects coins.	______________.
/aw/	Howard	Mr. Bowers	Mr. Crowley	Mr. Powell
	______________.	grows flowers.	______________.	photographs clouds.
/ay/	Kyle	Diane	Mike	Tyler
	flies kites.	______________.	is a library guide.	______________.

Complete each of the interview questions below in any way that you wish.
Some suggested words and phrases are shown below. Then interview a
partner and record his or her answers to your questions. The underlined words
contain diphthongs; be sure to pronounce the diphthongs correctly.

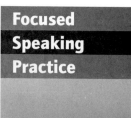

Suggested words and phrases

/ɔy/	/ay/	/aw/
a t**oy** for a child	wasting t**i**me	a h**ou**se / your h**ou**se
a ch**oi**ce you made	wr**i**ting	climbing a m**ou**ntain
making a ch**oi**ce	fr**i**ed r**i**ce	l**ou**d music
an old c**oi**n	sunsh**i**ne	p**ow**er
j**oi**ning a club	the r**i**ght answer	your t**ow**n

	Question	Answer
/ay/	1. Did you ever try...	*to write a novel?*
/ay/	2. Do you m**i**nd...	
/ay/	3. Did you ever b**uy**...	
/ay/	4. Do you l**i**ke...	
/ɔy /	5. Do you ever av**oi**d...	
/ɔy /	6. Are you ann**oy**ed by...	
/ɔy /	7. Do you enj**oy**...	
/aw/	8. Do you ever d**ou**bt...	
/aw/	9. Are you pr**ou**d of...	
/aw/	10. Have you ever f**ou**nd...	

Student B: Look at the chart below. Student A will work with the chart on page 70. Ask your partner questions to find out the hobbies that are missing for the people on your chart. Your partner will ask you similar questions to find out the hobbies that are missing from the chart on page 70.

Example:

Student A: What does Ms. Moyer do?

Student B: Ms. Moyer takes voice lessons. How about Roy? What does he do?

/ɔy/	Ms. M<u>oy</u>er	Ms. B<u>oy</u>d	R<u>oy</u>	Mrs. D<u>oy</u>le
	takes v<u>oi</u>ce lessons.	enj<u>oy</u>s needlepoint.	_____.	makes t<u>oy</u>s for b<u>oy</u>s.
/aw/	H<u>ow</u>ard	Mr. B<u>ow</u>ers	Mr. Cr<u>ow</u>ley	Mr. P<u>ow</u>ell
	likes l<u>ou</u>d music.	_____.	hangs <u>out</u> d<u>ow</u>nt<u>ow</u>n.	_____.
/ay/	K<u>y</u>le	D<u>i</u>ane	M<u>i</u>ke	T<u>y</u>ler
	_____.	r<u>i</u>des her b<u>i</u>ke for m<u>i</u>les.	_____.	l<u>i</u>kes to bake p<u>ie</u>s.

/iy/ as in s<u>ee</u>n and /ɪ/ as in d<u>i</u>d

The vowel sounds /iy/ and /ɪ/ are made by raising your tongue high in the front of your mouth. Make sure that you make /iy/ longer than /ɪ/ by gliding the /y/ sound at the end of /iy/.

/iy/

The lips are spread as if smiling.
The tongue is very high in the front of the mouth.
The jaw is slightly open.
The jaw and tongue glide to /y/ at the end.

Hint: Spread your lips into a smile as if someone is taking your picture.

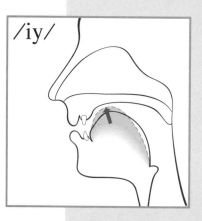

The /iy/ sound in cheese makes you look as though you are smiling.

Listen to examples of words with the /iy/ sound: fr<u>ee</u>, p<u>ea</u>s, m<u>e</u>, th<u>ie</u>f

/ɪ/

The lips are relaxed.
The tongue is high in the front of the mouth, but lower than /iy/.
The jaw is slightly open.

Listen to examples of words with the /ɪ/ sound: d<u>i</u>d, f<u>i</u>sh, pr<u>e</u>tty, b<u>u</u>sy

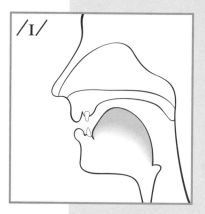

A. Listen to this poem and write in the missing words as you hear them. The first one is done for you.

The Silver Fish
by Shel Silverstein

	/iy/	/ɪ/

While (1) ___fishing___ in the blue lagoon   _____   _____

I caught a lovely (2) _____ fish,   _____   _____

And he spoke to me. "My boy," quoth (3) _____,   _____   _____

"(4) _____ set me free and I'll grant your   _____   _____

    wish...

A kingdom of (5) _____? A palace of   _____   _____

    gold?

Or all the goodies your fancies can hold?"

So I said, "OK," and I threw him (6) _____,   _____   _____

And he swam away and he laughed at me

Whispering my foolish (7) _____   _____   _____

Into a silent (8) _____.   _____   _____

Today I caught that (9) _____ again,   _____   _____

That lovely silver (10) _____ of fishes,   _____   _____

And once again he offered (11) _____ —   _____   _____

If only I would set him free —

Any one of a number of wonderful wishes...

He was (12) _____!   _____   _____

B. Listen to the pronunciation of the words you filled in. Put an X in the column for the vowel sound you hear in each word.

Now listen again and repeat after the speaker. Be careful to pronounce the /iy/ and /ɪ/ vowel sounds correctly.

Student A: You will work with this page. Student B will work with page 76. For each box below, circle either of the two words or phrases. Dictate these sentences to Student B, who will write down the words you say in the blanks on page 76. Then reverse roles. The phrases in the Word Box will help you with spelling.

My friend [Tr**i**na / Tr**i**sha] is a great cook. Everything she makes is

[del**i**cious / a tr**ea**t] . Yesterday we had [d**i**nner / a m**ea**l] at her house.

First, we had chips with [sour cr**ea**m / ch**ee**se] dip. Then she served a

[b**i**g / l**i**ttle] [gr**ee**n / C**ae**sar] salad with her famous [cr**ea**my / c**i**trus] dressing.

Word Box

veal
mixed vegetables
dill pickles
steamed

The main _____ was _____, and we also had

_____ and _____ _____.

Finally, she treated us to _____ for dessert.

Student B: You will work with this page. Student A will work with page 75. Listen to Student A. In the blanks below, write down the words Student A says. Next, for each box, circle one of the words or phrases. Dictate these sentences to Student A, who will write down the words you say in the blanks on page 75. The words in the Word Box will help you with spelling.

My friend _____ is a great cook. Everything she makes

is _____. Yesterday we had _____ at her

house. First, we had chips with _____ dip. Then

she served a _____ _____ salad with her

famous _____ dressing.

Word Box

Trina
Trisha
sour cream
Caesar
creamy
citrus

The main [d**i**sh / m**ea**l] was [ch**i**cken / b**ee**f / v**ea**l], and we also had

[m**i**xed vegetables / d**i**ll p**i**ckles] and [st**ea**med / gr**ee**n] [p**ea**s / b**ea**ns]. Finally, she

treated us to [ice cr**ea**m / p**ea**ches] for dessert.

With a group of four or five classmates, think of unusual uses for each of the following items. When it is your turn, tell the group what you will do with the item, and try to name all of your classmates' unusual uses as well. Be sure to pronounce the /iy/ and /ɪ/ sounds in these words correctly.

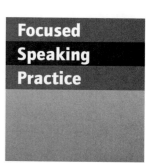

Example:

What will you do with a piece of string?

Alisha: I will tie the piece of string around my finger so I remember to do the dishes.

Brad: I will use the string to hang a picture on my wall, and Alisha will tie the string around her finger.

Carla: My cat and I will play with the string. Brad will use the string to hang a picture, and Alisha will tie the string around her finger.

What will you do with...

1. a p**ie**ce of str**i**ng
2. a l**i**ter of m**i**lk
3. a l**ea**ky t**ea**pot
4. a gr**ee**n bedsh**ee**t
5. a l**ea**f from a tr**ee**
6. thr**ee** w**i**shes
7. a pr**e**tty d**i**sh
8. l**i**ttle b**ea**ds on a str**i**ng
9. a b**i**g toy p**i**g
10. a p**ie**ce of m**ea**t

/ey/ as in pl<u>ay</u>, /ε/ as in s<u>e</u>nd, and /æ/ as in b<u>a</u>d

To make these sounds correctly, you must raise and lower your tongue in the front of your mouth. Also, pay attention to how far you must open your jaw, especially for the /æ/ sound.

/ey/

The lips are slightly spread.
The tongue is in the middle of the mouth in the front.
The jaw is slightly open.
The jaw and tongue move to /y/ at the end.

Listen to examples of words with the /ey/ sound: pl<u>ay</u>, s<u>a</u>me, r<u>ai</u>se, gr<u>ea</u>t

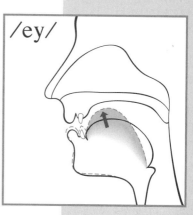

/ε/

The lips are slightly spread.
The tongue is in the middle of the mouth, lower than /ey/ but higher than /æ/.
The jaw is open.

Listen to examples of words with the /ε/ sound: s<u>e</u>nd, m<u>e</u>t, d<u>ea</u>d

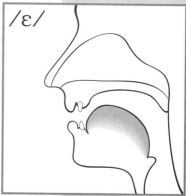

/æ/

The lips are open and relaxed.
The tongue is low in the front of the mouth.
The jaw is open wide.

Listen to examples of words with the /æ/ sound: b<u>a</u>d, c<u>a</u>n, s<u>a</u>t

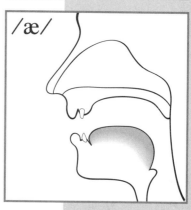

A. Listen to this conversation between a travel agent and a customer. Write in the missing words as you hear them. The first one is done for you.

Traveler: I want to **(1)** _*spend*_ a few **(2)** _____ in San Francisco.

Agent: I'd be **(3)** _____ to help you. What dates do you **(4)** _____ to travel?

Traveler: Saturday April **(5)** _____ to Monday the **(6)** _____ .

Agent: Do you want to fly or **(7)** _____ the train?

Traveler: If I can't **(8)** _____ an inexpensive plane ticket, I **(9)** _____ I could take the **(10)** _____ .

Agent: Let me **(11)** _____ some prices. **(12)** _____ I have your phone number? I'll call you this afternoon and tell you what I was **(13)** _____ to arrange.

Traveler: Sure. Here's my card. **(14)** _____ so much for all your **(15)** _____ .

B. Listen to the vowel sounds in these pairs of words. Some pairs have the same vowel sounds and some have different vowel sounds. Circle *same* or *different* to show which you hear. The first one is done for you.

1. same   (different)

2. same   different

3. same   different

4. same   different

5. same   different

6. same   different

7. same   different

8. same   different

Now listen to these pairs of words again and repeat after the speaker. Be careful to pronounce the /ey/, /ɛ/, and /æ/ sounds correctly.

Student A: Circle one of the two words in each sentence in the left column. Do not tell Student B which word you circled. Read the complete sentence to Student B.

Student B: Point to the picture that shows the meaning of the sentence Student A read.

After you and your partner have completed all the items, reverse roles and repeat the exercise.

1. Do you see the m**a**n / m**e**n?

2. Should we t**a**ste / t**e**st them?

3. He just l**au**ghed / l**e**ft.

4. They found a c**a**ne / c**a**n.

5. He has a d**a**te / d**e**bt.

6. Where is the p**ai**n / p**e**n / p**a**n?

A. Add one item to each of these lists of things people take on vacations. Make sure that each of your items has the correct sound.

/ey/	/ɛ/	/æ/
a r**a**dio	an umbr**e**lla	a m**a**p
a b**a**thing suit	a cr**e**dit card	a c**a**n opener
bug spr**ay**	a warm sw**ea**ter	a c**a**mera
writing p**a**per	a m**e**dicine kit	a fl**a**shlight
a p**ai**ntbrush	a t**e**nnis ball	sungl**a**sses
a r**ai**ncoat	a c**e**ll phone	m**a**tches
_____	_____	_____

B. With a group of classmates, discuss which five of these items you will take on

- a c**a**mping trip,
- beach vac**a**tion, or
- a drive across the d**e**sert

/ɑ/ as in n<u>o</u>t, /ow/ as in kn<u>ow</u>, and /aw/ as in br<u>ow</u>n

These three sounds are made by placing your tongue low in the back of your mouth. To make them sound different, pay attention to the lip placement and movement for each sound. /ɑ/ is often spelled with the letter o, so don't let the spelling fool you!

/ɑ/

The lips are open and relaxed.
The tongue is low in the center of the mouth.
The jaw is open wide.

Hint: This is the sound the doctor asks you to make when looking into your throat.

Listen to examples of words with the /ɑ/ sound: j<u>o</u>b, n<u>o</u>t, w<u>a</u>tch

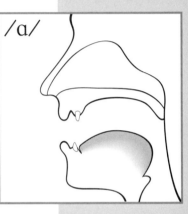

/aw/

Start with /ɑ/ and move to /w/.
The lips move from open and rounded to slightly closed and rounded.
The tongue moves from low in the center of the mouth to high in the back of the mouth.
The jaw rises.

Hint: This is a diphthong, so your mouth moves a lot when you say this sound.

Listen to examples of words with the /aw/ sound: n<u>ow</u>, br<u>ow</u>n, sh<u>ou</u>t

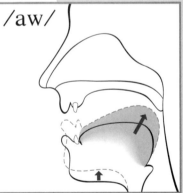

/ow/

The lips are open and rounded.
The tongue is in the middle of the mouth in the back.
The jaw is slightly open.
The lips move to /w/ at the end.

Listen to examples of words with the /ow/ sound: kn<u>ow</u>, ph<u>o</u>ne, b<u>oa</u>t

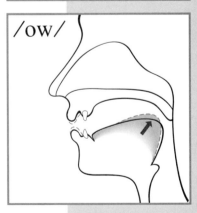

A. Listen to these answering machine messages. The missing words have one of the vowel sounds in this chapter. Write in the missing words as you hear them. The first one is done for you.

A: Hello. This is Claudia from **(1)** ___*Doctor*___ Townsend's

(2) _____. I'm **(3)** _____ to confirm your

appointment for tomorrow at four **(4)** _____.

B: This is Rhonda Brown from **(5)** _____ the street. I'll be

(6) _____ of **(7)** _____ this weekend. If you'll

be **(8)** _____, would you check for mail in our box and

keep an eye on our **(9)** _____?

C: Hi, it's Joan. I **(10)** _____ I left my **(11)** _____ at

your **(12)** _____ last night. If you've **(13)** _____

it, let me **(14)** _____. Thanks!

D: Hi. It's Bob. I **(15)** _____ by earlier. I **(16)** _____,

but I guess you weren't **(17)** _____. There's a

(18) _____ you might like this Friday, and I have

tickets. Let me **(19)** _____ if you'd like to

(20) _____ with me.

B. Listen to the vowel sounds in these groups of words. Mark the word whose vowel sound is different. The first one is done for you.

1. _____   _____   _✗_

2. _____   _____   _____

3. _____   _____   _____

4. _____   _____   _____

5. _____   _____   _____

6. _____   _____   _____

Now listen to these words again and repeat after the speaker. Be careful to pronounce the /ɑ/, /ow/, and /aw/ sounds correctly.

Student A: Put an X next to **one** phrase in each of the pairs in the left-hand column. Do not tell Student B which you marked. Read the phrase to Student B, being careful to pronounce the /ɑ/, /ow/, and /aw/ sounds correctly.

Student B: Listen to the phrase that Student A reads, and put an X next to the appropriate ending from the right-hand column.

After you and your partner have completed all six items, compare your answers. Then reverse roles and repeat the exercise.

1. _____ I thought I heard a sh**o**t,   _____ but it was a balloon popping.

    _____ I thought I heard a sh**ou**t.   _____ It was some children playing outside.

2. _____ She was f**o**nd   _____ of sweet desserts.

    _____ She was f**ou**nd   _____ hiding in her closet.

3. _____ It was hard to see **Da**wn   _____ because there were so many people.

    _____ It was hard to see d**ow**n   _____ to the end of the street.

4. _____ There was a kn**o**t   _____ in my shoelace that I couldn't untie.

    _____ There was a n**o**te   _____ on the table from his wife.

5. _____ They told the j**o**ck   _____ that he could play in Friday's game.

    _____ They told the j**o**ke   _____ and everyone laughed.

6. _____ I told him that I w**a**nt   _____ to have dinner at seven o'clock.

    _____ I told him that I w**o**n't   _____ be at home tonight.

With a partner, plan a dialog in which you call back the person who left each of the following messages. Present your dialog to the class and be sure to pronounce the /ɑ/, /aw/, and /ow/ sounds correctly.

Message 1: Hell**o**, dear. This is your f**a**ther. We haven't heard from you in a l**o**ng time, so we th**ou**ght we'd c**a**ll to say hell**o**. Your m**o**m and I w**a**nt to t**a**lk to you ab**ou**t moving back h**o**me to live with us. You could save some money, and we wouldn't be so l**o**nely. Give us a c**a**ll, OK?

Message 2: Hi… It's me. I just f**ou**nd **ou**t ab**ou**t a pr**o**blem at the **o**ffice, so I won't be h**o**me for dinner. I h**o**pe C**o**nnie and R**o**b aren't supposed to come **o**ver tonight. I've…uh…forg**o**tten when that is planned. I kn**ow** I was late last night too. Sorry…

Message 3: Hi, D**o**n. J**oe** and I are trying to find that restaurant you said to meet you at, but we haven't f**ou**nd it, and n**ow** we're l**o**st and can't get h**o**me. We're d**ow**nt**ow**n by some m**a**ll. C**a**ll me on my cell ph**o**ne. Soon!

Chapter 19

/ɑ/ as in n<u>o</u>t, /ʌ/ as in f<u>u</u>n, and /æ/ as in b<u>a</u>d

For these three sounds, the muscles of your tongue, lips, and jaw are very relaxed. Pay careful attention to the different tongue placement for each sound.

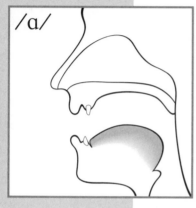

/ɑ/

The lips are open and relaxed.
The tongue is low in the center of the mouth.
The jaw is open wide.

Hint: **This is the sound the doctor asks you to make when looking into your throat.**

Listen to examples of words with the /ɑ/ sound: j<u>o</u>b, n<u>o</u>t, w<u>a</u>tch

Ahhh

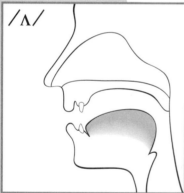

/ʌ/

The lips are relaxed.
The tongue is in the center of the mouth.
The jaw is relaxed.

Hint: **This sounds like schwa, but it is a stressed vowel. A schwa is unstressed.**

Listen to examples of words with the /ʌ/ sound: m<u>u</u>d, f<u>u</u>n, d<u>o</u>ne

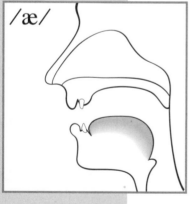

/æ/

The lips are open and relaxed.
The tongue is low in the front of the mouth.
The jaw is open.

Listen to examples of words with the /æ/ sound: b<u>a</u>d, c<u>a</u>n, s<u>a</u>t

A. Listen to two sports fans talk about their plans for the week. The missing words have one of the vowel sounds in this chapter. Write in the missing words as you hear them. The first one is done for you.

A: Do you **(1)** _____plan_____ to go to the Sonics game on Friday?

B: Sure. I just wish I had tickets for Tuesday's Blizzards

(2) _____!

A: You're in **(3)** _____. I have an extra — I have season

tickets — **(4)** _____ seats. My boyfriend and I are big

hockey **(5)** _____, but he has to go out of town because

of his **(6)** _____. Do you want to join me?

B: I'd **(7)** _____ to. By the way, this Monday my

(8) _____ is in the college **(9)** _____ meet.

A: Really? What's his event?

B: The long jump.

A: Monday, right? I'm **(10)** _____ it's not Wednesday. I

promised Pat I would come **(11)** _____ boxing on TV

that night.

B: Hey, I've been meaning to **(12)** _____ you, what are you

doing Saturday? We haven't **(13)** _____ golfing in a long

time.

A: You're right. Let's play at the country **(14)** _____ in

the morning.

B: Why **(15)** _____? It sounds like **(16)** _____!

A: See you there.

B. Listen to the vowel sounds in these pairs of words. Some pairs have the same vowel sounds and some have different vowel sounds. Circle *same* or *different* to show which you hear. The first one is done for you.

1. same   (different)

2. same   different

3. same   different

4. same   different

5. same   different

6. same   different

7. same   different

8. same   different

Now listen to these words again and repeat after the speaker. Be careful to pronounce the /ɑ/, /ʌ/, and /æ/ sounds correctly.

Student A: Put an X next to **one** phrase in each of the pairs in the left-hand column. Do not tell Student B which you marked. Read the phrase to Student B. Be careful to pronounce the /ɑ/, /ʌ/, and /æ/ sounds correctly.

Student B: Listen to the phrase that Student A reads, and put an X next to the appropriate ending from the right-hand column.

After you and your partner have completed all six items, compare your answers. Then reverse roles and repeat the exercise.

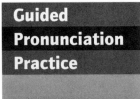

Guided
Pronunciation
Practice

1. _____ Did you notice the c**o**llar   _____ around the dog's neck?

    _____ Did you notice the c**o**lor   _____ of his car?

2. _____ She gave him a good l**u**ck   _____ kiss before he left.

    _____ She gave him a good l**o**ck   _____ to keep his bike secure.

3. _____ At the lake we saw a d**u**ck   _____ swimming with seven ducklings.

    _____ At the lake we saw a d**o**ck   _____ with three boats tied to it.

4. _____ Is that the l**a**st   _____ homework question?

    _____ Is that the l**o**st   _____ dog?

5. _____ We were pleased with the c**a**st   _____ of the theater production.

    _____ We were pleased with the c**o**st   _____ of our meal at that restaurant.

6. _____ They want to meet J**a**n   _____ and her sister.

    _____ They want to meet J**o**hn   _____ and his brother.

Work in a small group. Choose any two words from the list below and make a list of what those things have in common. Then choose two new words, and make a new list. Which group in your class can make the longest list?

Example:

a teacup and eyeglasses

- You can hold them both in your hand.
- They are both easily broken.
- People sometimes use them when they read the newspaper in the morning.

/æ/	/ʌ/	/ɑ/
an **a**pple	a teac**u**p	a st**o**p sign
eyegl**a**sses	a r**u**g	a b**o**ttle
a b**a**throbe	a gl**o**ve	a st**o**pw**a**tch
bl**a**ck shoes	a hairbr**u**sh	a flower p**o**t

/ɑ/ as in n<u>o</u>t and /ay/ as in fl<u>y</u>

For both of these sounds, the tongue starts in the same place. However, /ɑ/ is a short, quick sound, and /ay/ is a diphthong, so it is longer because the tongue moves from /ɑ/ to /y/.

/ɑ/

The lips are open and relaxed.
The tongue is low in the center of the mouth.
The jaw is open wide.

Hint: **This is the sound the doctor asks you to make when looking into your throat.**

Listen to examples of words with the /ɑ/ sound: j<u>o</u>b, n<u>o</u>t, w<u>a</u>tch

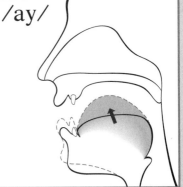

/ay/

Start with /ɑ/ and move to /y/.
The lips move from open and rounded to slightly closed and spread.
The tongue moves from low in the center of the mouth to high in the front of the mouth.
The jaw rises.

Hint: **This is a diphthong, so your mouth moves a lot when you say this sound.**

Listen to examples of words with the /ay/ sound: fl<u>y</u>, s<u>ig</u>n, r<u>ig</u>ht

A. Listen to these two friends talking about buying parts for their bicycles. The missing words have one of the vowel sounds in this chapter. Write in the missing words as you hear them. The first one is done for you.

A: My friend **(1)** _____ *Tom's* _____ bike was just stolen.

B: Did he report it to the police?

A: Yeah, but they said it's unlikely that they'll **(2)** _____ it.

B: I hear a lot of **(3)** _____ have been stolen lately. I don't know what I'd do if I lost my bike. I ride it all the

(4) _____. And to tell you the truth, I'm pretty

(5) _____ of it.

A: I need to buy a stronger **(6)** _____ for mine. Where's a good bike shop?

B: Stop by **(7)** _____ Bikes. I go there a

(8) _____. In fact, I just got a bike light there

(9) _____ long ago. It's **(10)** _____ of the

(11) _____.

A: I should get a **(12)** _____ too so I can ride at

(13) _____.

B: I have mine right here. See, it's still in the **(14)** _____. If you **(15)** _____ this one, you might want to get the same **(16)** _____.

B. Listen to these words, and circle the word that you hear. The first one is done for you.

1. (top)   type

2. fond   find

3. lot   light

4. Tom   time

5. lock   like

6. Lon   line

7. not   night

8. bikes   box

Now listen to these words again and repeat after the speaker. Be careful to pronounce the /ɑ/ and /ay/ sounds correctly.

Guided Pronunciation Practice
Student A

Student A: Look at the chart below. Student B will work with the chart on page 100. Ask your partner questions to find out what each person wanted to buy. Your partner will ask you similar questions using the chart on page 100.

Example:

Student A: Why did Todd go shopping?

Student B: He wanted to buy hot dogs.

/ɑ/	Todd	Don	Molly	Robin
	hot dogs	broccoli	____________	socks
/ɑ/ and /ay/	Holly	Connie	Mike	Mariah
	a fine clock	____________	a bike lock	____________
/ay/	Tyler	Lyle	Brian	Ryan
	____________	five knives	____________	a nice necktie

With a group of classmates, choose one of the products below and plan a radio commercial that advertises this product. Add any information you would like. Be careful to pronounce the vowel sounds /ɑ/ and /ay/ correctly.

The problem people have	The product	How the product solves this problem
Are you tired from working at a stressful job?	Stress Stopper Vitamins	Take them in times when you have a lot of stress in your life. They give your body a shot of energy.
What can you do if you don't have time to keep your body healthy by eating right?	The Smiling Diner	Hot, healthy meals are dropped off at your home five days a week. This saves time and helps you keep your body in top shape.
Is your eyesight not very good at night?	Fine Eyes Spotlight	A small pocket-sized flashlight that shines brightly to help you see at night.

Student B: Look at the chart below. Student A will work with the chart on page 98. Ask your partner questions to find out what each person wanted to buy. Your partner will ask you similar questions using the chart on page 98.

Example:

Student A: Why did Todd go shopping?

Student B: Todd wanted to buy hot dogs.

/ɑ/	Todd	Don	Molly	Robin
	hot dogs	_____	jogging shoes	_____
/ɑ/ and /ay/	Holly	Connie	Mike	Mariah
	_____	diet soda	_____	a chocolate pie
/ay/	Tyler	Lyle	Brian	Ryan
	rice	_____	a china teapot	_____

Chapter 21

/ow/ as in kn<u>ow</u>, /ɔ/ as in s<u>aw</u>, and /ʌ/ as in f<u>u</u>n

To make these sounds, your tongue will be in the middle or the back of your mouth. Be careful to round the lips for /ow/ and /ɔ/.

/ow/

The lips are open and rounded.
The tongue is in the middle of the mouth in the back.
The jaw is slightly open.
The lips move to /w/ at the end.

Listen to examples of words with the /ow/ sound: kn<u>ow</u>, ph<u>o</u>ne, v<u>o</u>te

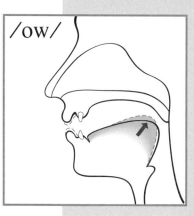

/ɔ/

The lips are slightly rounded.
The tongue is low in the back of the mouth.
The jaw is slightly open.

Listen to examples of words with the /ɔ/ sound: s<u>aw</u>, f<u>o</u>r, b<u>ou</u>ght

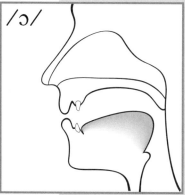

/ʌ/

The lips are relaxed.
The tongue is in the center of the mouth.
The jaw is relaxed.

Hint: This sounds like schwa, but it is a stressed vowel. A schwa is unstressed.

Listen to examples of words with the /ʌ/ sound: m<u>u</u>d, f<u>u</u>n, d<u>o</u>ne

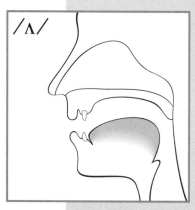

A. Listen to this presentation about human personality. The missing words have the vowel sounds you are studying in this chapter. Write in the missing words as you hear them. The first one is done for you.

Are our personalities **(1)** _*formed*_ by the people we know and the things we experience as we **(2)** _____ up? Or, do our genes carry the code for our personality? These are common questions in the study of psychology.

(3) _____ psychologists at the University of Minnesota wanted to **(4)** _____ the answer to these questions, so they studied twins who were separated a **(5)** _____ time after they were born. These twins did not know **(6)** _____ another and grew up in different **(7)** _____. Of course, they looked **(8)** _____ the same. But the twins often had similar talents and skills also, like being able to **(9)** _____ well or being good at sports. Some twins had many things in common. But the researchers also **(10)** _____ that even many unrelated people shared opinions, likes and dislikes, and experiences. Why? Because **(11)** _____ of these people were the same age and from the same culture. So what affects personality the **(12)** _____? This research seems to **(13)** _____ that 20–45% of our personality **(14)** _____ from our parents. So, our age, culture, and experiences probably affect our personalities as **(15)** _____ as our genes do — maybe even **(16)** _____!

B. Listen to the vowel sounds in these pairs of words. Some pairs have the same vowel sound and some have different vowel sounds. Circle *same* or *different* to show which you hear. The first one is done for you.

1. same   (different)

2. same   different

3. same   different

4. same   different

5. same   different

6. same   different

7. same   different

8. same   different

Now listen to these words again and repeat after the speaker. Be careful to pronounce the /ow/, /ɔ/, and /ʌ/ sounds correctly.

Student A: Put an X next to **one** phrase in each of the pairs in the left-hand column. Do not tell Student B which phrase you marked. Read the phrase to Student B, being careful to pronounce the /ow/, /ɔ/, and /ʌ/ sounds correctly.

Student B: Listen to the phrase that Student A reads, and put an X next to the appropriate ending from the right-hand column.

After you and your partner have completed all six items, compare your answers. Then reverse roles and repeat the exercise.

1. _____ I never s**ew**   _____ on buttons. I don't know how.

   _____ I never s**aw**   _____ that man before.

2. _____ Do you think the l**aw**n   _____ needs to be mowed?

   _____ Do you think the l**oa**n   _____ can be paid off in a year?

3. _____ You have to pay the t**o**ll   _____ to drive on this road.

   _____ You have to pay the t**a**ll   _____ man for anything you buy in this store.

4. _____ We are expecting a f**u**n   _____ vacation in the mountains.

   _____ We are expecting a ph**o**ne   _____ call from our friend.

5. _____ You need to c**u**t   _____ the loose thread off your sleeve.

   _____ You need to c**oa**t   _____ the chicken in breadcrumbs; then fry it.

6. _____ These n**u**ts   _____ would be good in cookies.

   _____ These n**o**tes   _____ sound a little bit flat.

Look at the following list of personality traits that contain the vowel sounds from this chapter. Choose another trait and add it to the last space in the chart. Mark the box that will make a true statement about you.

Ask others in your class about their choices. Whose personality is most similar to yours? Whose personality is very different?

	I am very...	I am a little...	I am not...
/ow/			
Em<u>o</u>tional	_____	_____	_____
M<u>o</u>tivated	_____	_____	_____
S<u>o</u>cial	_____	_____	_____
/ɔ/			
Th<u>ou</u>ghtful	_____	_____	_____
<u>O</u>rganized	_____	_____	_____
C<u>au</u>tious	_____	_____	_____
/ʌ/			
F<u>u</u>nny	_____	_____	_____
L<u>u</u>cky	_____	_____	_____
St<u>u</u>bborn	_____	_____	_____
_____	_____	_____	_____

/ɔy/ as in c<u>oi</u>n, /ɑ/* as in n<u>o</u>t, and /ɔ/ as in s<u>aw</u>

To make these three sounds, your tongue must be low in your mouth. Pay attention to the difference in how wide your mouth is open for each sound.

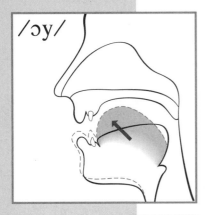

/ɔy/

Start with /ɔ/ and move to /y/.
The lips move from closed and rounded to slightly closed and spread.
The tongue moves from low in the back of the mouth to high in the front of the mouth.
The jaw rises.

Hint: **This is a diphthong, so your mouth moves a lot when you say this sound.**

Listen to examples of words with the /ɔy/ sound: b<u>oy</u>, c<u>oin</u>, m<u>oi</u>st

/ɑ/

The lips are open and relaxed.
The tongue is low in the center of the mouth.
The jaw is open wide.

Ahhh

Hint: **This is the sound the doctor asks you to make when looking into your throat.**

Listen to examples of words with the /ɑ/ sound: j<u>o</u>b, n<u>o</u>t, w<u>a</u>tch

/ɔ/

The lips are slightly rounded.
The tongue is low in the back of the mouth.
The jaw is slightly open.

Listen to examples of words with the /ɔ/ sound: s<u>aw</u>, f<u>or</u>, b<u>ou</u>ght

*In some dialects of American English, /ɔ/ and /ɑ/ are often pronounced the same way.

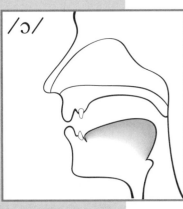

A. Listen to this excerpt from a cooking show. The missing words have the vowel sounds from this chapter. Write in the missing words as you hear them. The first one is done for you.

Today on Joyful Cooking, we'll make a quick, easy meal for

(1) ___four___.

First we're making lamb **(2)** _____. I bake them in a

medium **(3)** _____ oven. Be sure to cover the

(4) _____ with **(5)** _____ to keep the chops

(6) _____. I like to add a little **(7)** _____

(8) _____ to my lamb chops. In the last few minutes

we'll **(9)** _____ them until they're a little brown on

(10) _____.

Now, we'll prepare the vegetables. **(11)** _____ some

(12) _____ into the wok. Let the oil get pretty

(13) _____, but don't let it burn. Now, sauté the

vegetables until they're just a little soft when you test them with

a **(14)** _____. Add some salt, and your favorite sauce or

some lemon juice, and **(15)** _____!

B. Listen to the pronunciation of these words. Place each word in the column for the vowel sound it contains. The first one is done for you.

/ɔy/ as in coin	/ɑ/ as in not	/ɔ/ as in bought
1. _____	_____	___*four*___
2. _____	_____	_____
3. _____	_____	_____
4. _____	_____	_____
5. _____	_____	_____
6. _____	_____	_____
7. _____	_____	_____
8. _____	_____	_____
9. _____	_____	_____
10. _____	_____	_____
11. _____	_____	_____
12. _____	_____	_____

Now listen to these words again and repeat after the speaker. Be careful to pronounce the /ɔy/, /ɑ/, and /ɔ/ sounds correctly.

Student A: You will work with this page. Student B will work with page 110. For each box below, circle either of the two words or phrases. Dictate these sentences to Student B, who will write down the words you say in the blanks on page 110. Then reverse roles. The phrases in the Word Box will help you with spelling.

Everyone is different.

| Joyce / Troy | and | Scott / Roger | love to watch | hockey / soccer | , |

but | Paul / Lloyd | doesn't. He thinks this sport is

| noisy / annoying | and | awful / boring | .

He is more _____. Instead, he enjoys

_____. Shopping is _____

hobby. Today she went to the _____ and _____

some _____.

Word Box

thoughtful
cautious
collecting coins
taking voice
    lessons
popular rock
    albums

Student B: You will work with this page. Student A will work with page 109. Listen to Student A. In the blanks below, write down the words Student A says. Next, for each box, circle either of the two words or phrases. Dictate these sentences to Student A, who will write down the words you say in the blanks on page 109. The words in the Word Box will help you with spelling.

Everyone is different.

_____ and _____ love to watch _____,

but _____ doesn't. He thinks this sport is

_____ and _____ .

Word Box

Joyce
Troy
Scott
Roger
Paul
Lloyd
annoying

He is more | thoughtful / cautious | . Instead, he enjoys

| collecting coins / taking voice lessons | . Shopping is | my daughter's / my mom's | hobby.

Today she went to the | store / mall | and | bought / got | some

| small toys / popular rock albums | .

These words are typically used in recipes, and have the vowel sounds /ɔy/, /ɑ/, and /ɔ/.

Cooking words:

/ɔy/   b**oi**l, br**oi**l, ch**oi**ce, m**oi**sten, f**oi**l

/ɑ/   br**o**th, ch**o**p, diss**o**lve, dr**o**p, s**au**ce, t**o**p, t**o**ss, w**a**sh, w**o**k

/ɔ/   f**o**rk, p**ou**r, s**au**té, st**o**re, th**aw**, w**a**rm

Look for these words in the following example. Then tell a group of your classmates about a real or imaginary recipe. You can make up an unusual or interesting recipe using any ingredients you would like. Use the words from the list above and other words with the vowel sounds /ɔy/, /ɑ/, and /ɔ/.

Example recipe:

T**o**ssed Salad

Ch**o**p one head of lettuce, two tomatoes, and two sm**a**ll onions.

W**a**sh two carrots and f**ou**r radishes. Remove the green t**o**ps of the carrots and radishes and peel the carrots bef**o**re slicing them and adding them to the salad.

T**o**ss with **o**live **oi**l and vinegar until m**oi**stened.

/uw/ as in bl<u>ue</u>, /ʊ/ as in sh<u>ou</u>ld, and /ʌ/ as in f<u>u</u>n

For /uw/ and /ʊ/, your tongue is high in the back of the mouth. Be sure to add the /w/ glide to /uw/ and make it longer than /ʊ/. For /ʌ/, the tongue is in the center of your mouth. This sound is often spelled with a letter *u*, but don't let the spelling fool you.

/uw/

The lips are tightly rounded.
The tongue is very high in the back of the mouth.
The jaw is slightly open.
The lips move to /w/ at the end.

Listen to examples of words with the /uw/ sound: bl<u>ue</u>, m<u>oo</u>d, j<u>ui</u>ce, y<u>ou</u>

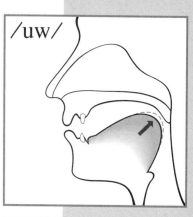

/ʊ/

The lips are rounded.
The tongue is high in the back of the mouth, but lower than /uw/.
The jaw is slightly open.

Listen to examples of words with the /ʊ/ sound: sh<u>ou</u>ld, p<u>u</u>t, t<u>oo</u>k

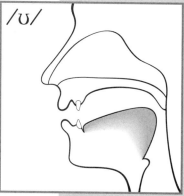

/ʌ/

The lips are relaxed.
The tongue is in the center of the mouth.
The jaw is relaxed.

Hint: **This sounds like schwa, but it is a stressed vowel. A schwa is unstressed.**

Listen to examples of words with the /ʌ/ sound: m<u>u</u>d, f<u>u</u>n, d<u>o</u>ne

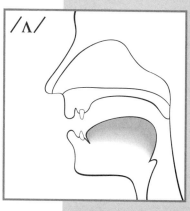

A. Listen to this student ask a friend for advice. The missing words have the vowel sounds from this chapter. Write in the missing words as you hear them. The first one is done for you.

A: Do you have a minute? I **(1)** _____*could*_____ really use your input.

B: Sure. What's **(2)** _____?

A: I'm having some **(3)** _____ in one of my classes. I took it because I thought it **(4)** _____ be easy, but it's really tough. I've studied every page of the **(5)** _____, but I still can't get a good grade on the exams.

B: Can you drop the class?

A: It's too late to do that. What do you think I **(6)** _____ do?

B: Hmm... That's bad **(7)** _____. When's the next test?

A: It's **(8)** _____. Next Tuesday.

B: Maybe the professor can suggest some **(9)** _____ ways for you to study. Have you talked to him? Her?

A: Him. No. I'd feel like a **(10)** _____.

B: He won't think you're a fool. He'll probably be glad you're trying to improve. **(11)** _____ tell him how hard you've been studying and ask what you should do. When are his office hours?

A: Tomorrow at **(12)** _____.

B: **(13)** _____. If I were you, I would go. What have you got to **(14)** _____?

B. Listen to the vowel sounds in these pairs of words. Some pairs have the same vowel sound and some have different vowel sounds. Circle *same* or *different* to show which you hear. The first one is done for you.

1. (same)   different

2. same   different

3. same   different

4. same   different

5. same   different

6. same   different

7. same   different

8. same   different

9. same   different

10. same   different

Now listen to these words again and repeat after the speaker. Be careful to pronounce the /uw/, /ʊ/, and /ʌ/ sounds correctly.

Student A: Put an X next to **one** phrase in each of the pairs in the left-hand column. Do not tell Student B which you marked. Read the phrase to Student B, being careful to pronounce the /uw/, /ʊ/, and /ʌ/ sounds correctly.

Student B: Listen to the phrase that Student A reads, and put an X next to the appropriate ending from the right-hand column.

After you and your partner have completed all six items, compare your answers. Then reverse roles and repeat the exercise.

1. _____ I think he's a f**oo**l   _____ if he buys that expensive car.
   _____ I think he's a f**u**ll   _____ professor, but I'm not sure.

2. _____ They suggested that we p**oo**l   _____ our resources and work together.
   _____ They suggested that we p**u**ll   _____ a trailer behind our car.

3. _____ We knew if we st**ew**ed   _____ the meat it would taste better.
   _____ We knew if we st**oo**d   _____ long enough, our legs would get tired.

4. _____ He needs to borrow a b**oo**k   _____ to write his research paper.
   _____ He needs to borrow a b**u**ck   _____ to buy himself a drink.

5. _____ You have to p**u**tt   _____ the golf ball into the hole.
   _____ You have to p**u**t   _____ your signature right here.

6. _____ She always l**u**cks into   _____ money.
   _____ She always l**oo**ks into   _____ new companies before investing.

Read these problems and the suggestions that follow. Choose the suggestion that you think is best, or add another suggestion of your own. Discuss your answers in a small group, and explain why you think the suggestion you chose is good advice. Be careful to pronounce the /uw/, /ʊ/, and /ʌ/ vowel sounds correctly.

Problem 1: I took a tough class, and I haven't done well on the first two tests. I want to get a good grade. What should I do to improve?

a. You could find a buddy in class who will study the book with you.

b. I would ask the instructor if I could come to his or her office after school for extra help.

c. You should drop the class. Choose a new class next term.

d. _____

Problem 2: I'm having trouble with my roommate. She uses my stuff and cooks my food without asking. I would like to move, but it's too expensive.

a. You worry too much. You should use her stuff and cook her food too. She shouldn't mind.

b. I would put a label on all my food saying "Don't touch."

c. You could ask your roommate to help make some rules that you both must follow.

d. _____

Problem 3: I have to choose a major soon. I'm not sure what I should study.

a. Think about classes that you took and loved. Your favorite class would make a good major.

b. I would choose a major where I could make good money.

c. You could use the school's catalog and choose anything that looks fun. You can always choose a new major later.

d. _____

Consonants are the sounds you make by touching different parts of your mouth, such as your lips, tongue, teeth, and different places on the roof of your mouth, or by bringing these parts of the mouth very close together. The chart on the next page shows which parts of your mouth you use to make English sounds.

Tip

Remember the process of learning a new sound: First, you must learn to hear the sound correctly, so practice listening. Next, you must learn how to make the sound using your mouth, tongue, and lips. Then you must practice making the sound and building up your mouth muscles. Finally, you need to practice making the sound correctly in your everyday speech. This process may take several weeks — or longer — but you can master the pronunciation if you practice every day.

If your native language does not have a certain consonant sound, you might find it difficult to say the sound in English because the muscles in your mouth and tongue are not used to forming the sound. You should not plan on using every chapter in Part Four. Only choose the chapters that focus on sounds that are difficult for you. If you aren't sure which sounds give you trouble, take the diagnostic test on the *Sound Bites* website.

	Two lips	Top teeth & bottom lip	Tongue tip & teeth	Tongue tip & upper gum	Tongue front & top of mouth	Tongue in the center	Tongue back & back of mouth	Throat
Nasal	m			n			ŋ	
Stop	p b			t d			k g	
Fricative		f v	θ ð	s z	ʃ ʒ			h
Stop & Fricative					tʃ dʒ			
Glides	w			r	y	r	w	
Sides of tongue				l				

Voiced sounds are made by vibrating the vocal cords. All vowels and many consonants are voiced. Voiceless sounds are made without vibrating the vocal cords. Listen to the example sentence, first spoken normally, and then whispered. When it is whispered, all of its sounds are voiceless.

English has fifteen vowel sounds and twenty-four consonant sounds.

To feel this difference, place your hand on your throat, and say the example sentence: First, say it normally. Then whisper it. Whispering is voiceless, and you should feel no vocal chord vibration when you whisper.

Don't worry if you aren't able to pronounce these sounds correctly; you will practice them again in later chapters. For now, just make sure you understand the difference between voiced and voiceless sounds.

All vowels are voiced: iy, ɪ, ɛ, ey, æ, ʌ, ɑ, uw, ʊ, ɔ, ow, ə, ɔy, ay, aw.

Voiced consonants: b, m, w, v, n, d, z, l, r, ð, ʒ, dʒ, y, g, ŋ.

Voiceless consonants: p, f, t, s, θ, ʃ, tʃ, k, h.

A. Listen to these sounds and the words that begin with the sounds. The first sound in each word is made in exactly the same way, except one is voiceless and the other is voiced. Put your hand on your throat and repeat the sounds and words after you hear them.

Voiceless sounds		Voiced sounds	
1. /p/	pat	/b/	bat
2. /f/	few	/v/	view
3. /t/	tear	/d/	dear
4. /s/	Sue	/z/	zoo
5. /tʃ/	choke	/dʒ/	joke
6. /k/	cap	/g/	gap
7. /θ/	think	/ð/	this

B. Look at the pairs of words marked in the sentences below. One word in each pair starts with a voiced sound and the other word starts with a voiceless sound. If you think the first sound in the word is voiced, write a *V* above the word. If you think the first sound is voiceless, write *VL* above the word. Then listen to the recording to check your predictions.

1. **J**ane's **ch**ain is in her **b**ack**p**ack.

2. There's a **f**ine **v**ine growing on **K**ate's **g**ate.

3. The list of things **t**o **d**o is in **Z**ach's **s**ack.

Listen to these sentences again and repeat after the speaker. Be careful to pronounce the voiced and voiceless sounds correctly.

Student A: Put an X next to **one** sentence in each of the pairs in the left-hand column. Do not tell Student B which you marked. Read the sentence to Student B.

Student B: Point to the picture that shows the meaning of the sentence that Student A read.

After you and your partner have completed all six items, compare your answers. Then reverse roles and repeat the exercise.

1. _____ It's a picture of a **f**ace.
   _____ It's a picture of a **v**ase.

2. _____ She gave him the **p**ill.
   _____ She gave him the **b**ill.

3. _____ I like the blue **ch**aise.
   _____ I like the blue **j**ays.

4. _____ **S**ip it carefully.
   _____ **Z**ip it carefully.

5. _____ We saw the **c**oat.
   _____ We saw the **g**oat.

6. _____ What cute **t**ots.
   _____ What cute **d**ots.

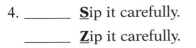
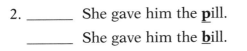

Focused Speaking Practice

Make a list of ten words that begin with consonants. Put a *V* next to the words that begin with voiced consonants. Put *VL* next to words that begin with voiceless consonants. Read your words to a partner. As you read each word, your partner will circle *voiced* or *voiceless* to show what kind of consonant the word begins with. Compare your answers. Then switch roles and do the same for your partner's words.

V / VL   **Your words**

1. _____   _____

2. _____   _____

3. _____   _____

4. _____   _____

5. _____   _____

6. _____   _____

7. _____   _____

8. _____   _____

9. _____   _____

10. _____   _____

Your partner's words

1. Voiced   Voiceless

2. Voiced   Voiceless

3. Voiced   Voiceless

4. Voiced   Voiceless

5. Voiced   Voiceless

6. Voiced   Voiceless

7. Voiced   Voiceless

8. Voiced   Voiceless

9. Voiced   Voiceless

10. Voiced   Voiceless

/r/ as in <u>r</u>ed and /l/ as in <u>l</u>ight

Some students of English confuse the /r/ and /l/ sounds. Other students make an /r/ sound that differs from the English /r/ sound. If these sounds are difficult for you, you may need to practice daily for several weeks to make the muscles in your tongue strong enough to say the new sound.

"I said, hamburger with *fries*."

/r/

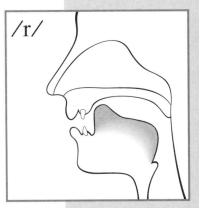

/r/

The sides of the tongue touch the sides of the teeth.
The tip of the tongue may curl up, but it does not touch anything.
Air flows over the tongue.
/r/ is voiced.

Listen to examples of words with the /r/ sound: <u>r</u>ed, bo<u>rr</u>ow, doo<u>r</u>

Other spelling patterns: <u>wr</u>ite

/l/

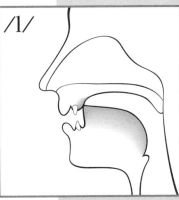

/l/

The tip of the tongue touches the gum behind the top teeth.
Air flows around the side of the tongue.
/l/ is voiced.*

Listen to examples of words with the /l/ sound: <u>l</u>ight, si<u>ll</u>y, mi<u>l</u>e

*When /l/ comes at the end of a word, the tongue is raised in the back of the mouth to touch the soft palate and the front to touch the alveolar ridge. This is sometimes called a "dark" /l/ and has a slightly different sound than the /l/ in the beginning and middle of words.

A. Listen to this conversation between two friends who are planning a party. Write in the missing words as you hear them. The first one is done for you.

A: Did you know that Friday is Rhonda's birthday?

B: We should have a **(1)** _surprise_ party for her! Maybe we could have a costume party.

A: But if it's a surprise, Rhonda won't have a costume.

B: We could bring a **(2)** _____, and she could be the queen of the party.

A: We only have a few days, and I think it's too **(3)** _____ to plan a costume party. You just want to wear that **(4)** _____ costume of yours!

B: OK. OK. You're right. But I **(5)** _____ it to Ray, so let's just have a picnic at the park on Edison **(6)** _____.

A: Yeah, that's a **(7)** _____ nice park, but we need to have it early enough that it'll still be **(8)** _____ outside.

B: Right. Friday's a workday. We'll have to have get together **(9)** _____ after work.

A: OK. Let's make a list of the **(10)** _____ that we'll need, and I'll go shopping.

B: You know, there's only one thing **(11)** _____ with this plan.

A: What's that?

B: I think it's supposed to **(12)** _____ on Friday.

A: Oh, no. Hmm… Maybe we could **(13)** _____ a room at the restaurant that Rick manages. They have a private room in the **(14)** _____ .

B: He might be able to give us a good **(15)** _____ . But, we'd better not wait too **(16)** _____ to call him.

A: You're right. I'll do it now.

B. Listen to these sentences and circle the word that you hear. The first one is done for you.

1. You should take the (right) / light box.

2. Did you bring the surp<u>r</u>ise / supp<u>l</u>ies?

3. I think we took the **<u>wr</u>ong** / <u>l</u>ong road.

4. The child wanted to see the c<u>r</u>own / c<u>l</u>own.

5. He said it was the rea<u>r</u> / rea<u>l</u> one.

6. Don't stand in the <u>r</u>ain / <u>l</u>ane.

7. Can we pay that <u>r</u>ate / <u>l</u>ate?

8. Did you say "<u>r</u>ent" / "<u>l</u>ent"?

Listen to these sentences again and repeat after the speaker. Be sure to pronounce the /r/ and /l/ sounds correctly.

Guided Pronunciation Practice
Student A

Student A: Look at the chart below. Student B will work with the chart on page 130. Ask your partner questions to find out where the people on your chart live. Your partner will ask you similar questions to find out where people live.

Example:

Student A: Where does Rita live?

Student B: Rita lives on Rocky Glen Road.

/r/	Rita	Rebecca	Robbie	Ryan
	______	Rose Ridge Place	______	Richardson Street
/r/ and /l/	Laura	Larry	Rosa	Robin
	Redwood Loop	______	Randolph Lane	______
/l/	Leslie	Lee	Lucas	Lisa
	______	Locust Avenue	______	Laurel Place

Guided Pronunciation Practice
Student B

Student B: Look at the chart below. Student A will work with the chart on page 129. Ask your partner questions to find out where the people on your chart live. Your partner will ask you similar questions to find out where people live.

Example:

Student A: Where does Rita live?

Student B: Rita lives on Rocky Glen Road.

/r/	Rita	Rebecca	Robbie	Ryan
	Rocky Glen Road	____________	Wren Street	____________
/r/ and /l/	Laura	Larry	Rosa	Robin
	____________	Larkin Street	____________	Lincoln Circle
/l/	Leslie	Lee	Lucas	Lisa
	Lyon Place	____________	Hillcrest Way	____________

Choose a spot on the map below and mark it with an X. Pretend that this X marks the place where your home is located. With a partner, practice giving directions. Your partner will give you a location on the map, and you should give directions from that location to your home.

Example:

A: I'm at the laundromat on Rose Lane.

B: Ok. Go down Rose Lane until you get to the railroad tracks...

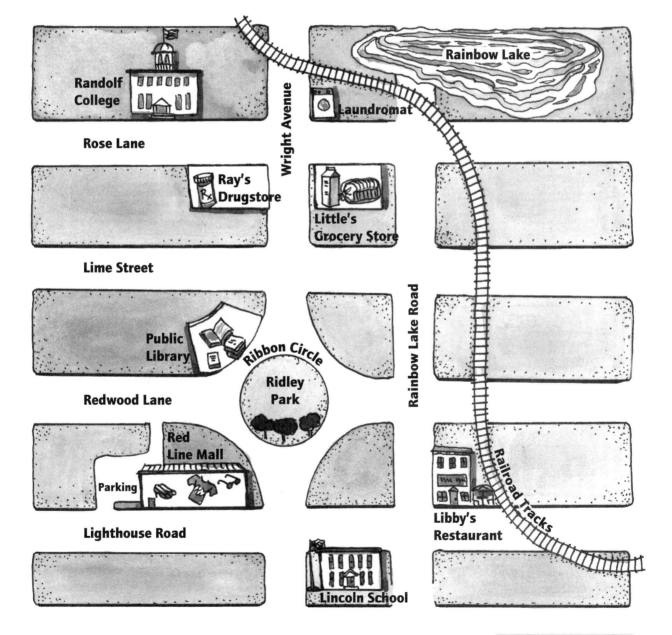

/θ/ as in <u>th</u>ing and /ð/ as in <u>th</u>at

These two sounds are made by pushing air between the tongue and the front teeth. As you practice this sound, try to feel the space between your front teeth with the tip of your tongue.

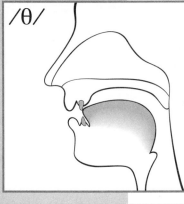

/θ/

The tip of the tongue is close to the top teeth.
Air flows between the tongue and teeth.
/θ/ is voiced.

Listen to examples of words with the /θ/ sound: <u>th</u>ing, au<u>th</u>or, bo<u>th</u>

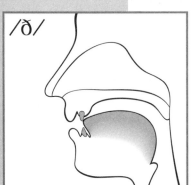

/ð/

The tip of the tongue is close to the top teeth.
Air flows between the tongue and teeth.
/ð/ is voiceless.

Listen to examples of words with the /ð/ sound: <u>th</u>at, clo<u>th</u>ing, brea<u>the</u>

The *th* sounds are easily confused with other English sounds. Watch out for these errors:

Don't confuse /θ/ as in *thank* with /t/ as in *tank*
or /ð/ as in *they* with /d/ as in *day*.

Don't confuse /θ/ as in *thing* with /s/ as in *sing*
or /ð/ as in *then* with /z/ as in *Zen*.

Don't confuse /θ/ as in *three* with /f/ as in *free*
or /ð/ as in *though* with /ʃ/ as in *show*.

A. Listen to this talk about Anthony's family. As you listen, fill in this family tree showing each of Anthony's relatives. Put in their names, their professions or accomplishments, and their relationships to Anthony. One is done for you.

Grandfather Timothy went to _____ Pole	Grandmother Edith went to South Pole		_____ Arthur _____ on law and _____	Grandmother Ruth dentist — false _____

_____ Keith _____ _____	Mother Martha _____ of *thirty* novels	Aunt Katherine actress in the _____

Anthony	_____ Matthew had triplets	Sister-in-law Cathy had triplets

_____	_____	_____

B. Retell the story of Anthony's family to a partner using the completed chart as a guide. Be sure to pronounce the *th* sounds correctly.

C. Listen to these sentences and circle the word that you hear. The first one is done for you.

1. Did you find a free pass /(pa**th**?)

2. He has a big mouse / mou**th**.

3. It was closing / clo**th**ing.

4. Did you say "day" / "**th**ey?"

5. There are tree / **th**ree houses.

6. They gave us free / **th**ree tickets.

7. They fought / **th**ought all afternoon.

8. Is that what she taught / **th**ought?

9. How do you spell wish / wi**th**?

10. The baby has to tee**th**e / two tee**th**.

Listen to these sentences again and repeat after the speaker. Be sure to pronounce the *th* sounds correctly.

Student A: Look at the date book on this page. Try to find an afternoon or evening before the big test when you and Student B could study together. Assume you are both busy at work or school every morning. Student B will look at the date book on page 136.

Example:

Student A: Do you have time to study on Monday, March 3rd?

Student B: In the evening?

Student A: No. I'm going to the theater in the evening. Are you free in the afternoon?

Student B: No. I have physical therapy. What are you doing on Tuesday?

Monday	March 3rd		Thursday	March 6th
Morning:			Morning:	
Afternoon:			Afternoon:	
Evening: *go to the theater*			Evening:	

Tuesday	March 4th		Friday	March 7th
Morning:			Morning: *THE BIG TEST!!!*	
Afternoon:			Afternoon:	
Evening: *help father bathe his dog*			Evening:	

Wednesday	March 5th		Saturday/Sunday	March 8th/9th
Morning:			Morning:	
Afternoon: *Math class*			Afternoon:	
Evening:			Evening:	

Student B: Look at the date book on this page. Try to find an afternoon or evening before the big test when you and Student A could study together. Assume you are both busy at work or school every morning. Student A will look at the date book on page 135.

Example:

Student A: Do you have time to study on Monday, March 3rd?

Student B: In the evening?

Student A: No. I'm going to the theater in the evening. Are you free in the afternoon?

Student B: No. I have physical therapy. What are you doing on Tuesday?

Monday	March 3rd
Morning:	
Afternoon: *physical therapy*	
Evening:	

Tuesday	March 4th
Morning:	
Afternoon: *Math class*	
Evening:	

Wednesday	March 5th
Morning:	
Afternoon:	
Evening: *Clothing shopping with mother*	

Thursday	March 6th
Morning:	
Afternoon: *teeth cleaning at dentist*	
Evening:	

Friday	March 7th
Morning: *THE BIG TEST!!!*	
Afternoon:	
Evening:	

Saturday/Sunday	March 8th/9th
Morning:	
Afternoon:	
Evening:	

Create a story that uses as many words as possible that contain the *th* sound. You may use words from the following list, but be sure to add some words of your own. Record your story on audio tape or tell the story to a partner.

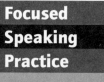

wea**th**er	**th**is / **th**at	**th**anks
toge**th**er	**th**ese / **th**ose	**th**under
ei**th**er	bo**th**	**th**ink
brea**th**e	**th**ermometer	pa**th**
clo**th**ing	**th**rough	**th**row
bro**th**er	**th**ick	mou**th**
there	**th**irsty	_____
_____	_____	_____
_____	_____	_____
_____	_____	_____
_____	_____	_____

/b/ as in <u>b</u>ig and /v/ as in <u>v</u>an

You use your bottom lip to make both of these sounds, but for /b/, both lips touch. For /v/, your top teeth must touch your bottom lip. When first practicing /v/, some students find it helpful to use their finger to hold the top lip away from the bottom lip until they can do it naturally.

/b/

The top lip touches the bottom lip.
Air is completely stopped and then released.
/b/ is voiced.

Listen to examples of words with the /b/ sound: <u>b</u>ig, ha<u>b</u>it, la<u>b</u>

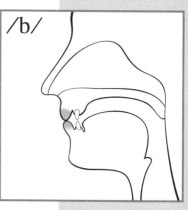

/v/

The top teeth are close to the bottom lip.
Air flows between the teeth and lip.
/v/ is voiced.

Listen to examples of words with the /v/ sound: <u>v</u>an, e<u>v</u>er, mo<u>v</u>e

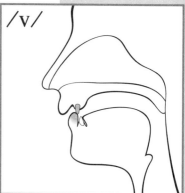

A. Listen to this presentation on the importance of eating fruits and vegetables. Write in the missing words as you hear them.

If you eat a balanced diet, your body will be stronger and you will feel and look your **(1)** ___*best*___. But, how can you be sure you're doing a good **(2)** _____ of eating the right foods? Eat **(3)** _____ healthy foods, including at least **(4)** _____ servings of fruits and vegetables each day. This is the best way to be sure you're giving your **(5)** _____ the vitamins and minerals it needs.

You can choose from a wide **(6)** _____ of fruits and vegetables. For example, leafy green vegetables like spinach and broccoli are **(7)** _____ good for your body. These vegetables are good for your **(8)** _____, your skin, and your blood **(9)** _____ they contain vitamins A, E, and K. Dried **(10)** _____ have lots of fiber and minerals, so they are a very healthy food. The potassium in bananas and potatoes is **(11)** _____ for your brain and nerves. The potatoes are **(12)** _____ for you if you eat them with the skins on. You should peel the **(13)** _____, of course!

You probably know that **(14)** _____ C is good for you. You can get it from many foods, including oranges, **(15)** _____, tomatoes, and broccoli. In fact, broccoli may be the healthiest vegetable there is. It also contains calcium, which is important for your **(16)** _____ and teeth. So it can be easy to make sure you eat right. Just choose your favorite fruits and vegetables and be sure to eat a lot of them!

B. Listen to the /b/ and /v/ sounds in these pairs of words. Some pairs have the same sound and some have different sounds. Circle *same* or *different* to show which you hear. Be careful! Sometimes, the /b/ and /v/ sounds come at the ends of the words. The first one is done for you.

1. same   (different)

2. same   different

3. same   different

4. same   different

5. same   different

6. same   different

7. same   different

8. same   different

Listen to these words again and repeat after the speaker. Be careful to pronounce the /b/ and /v/ sounds correctly.

Student A: Put an X next to **one** phrase in each of the pairs in the left-hand column. Do not tell Student B which you marked. Read the phrase to Student B.

Student B: Listen to the phrase that Student A reads, and put an X next to the appropriate ending from the right-hand column.

After you and your partner have completed all four items, compare your answers. Then reverse roles and repeat the exercise.

1. _____ Do you want a **v**ery red shirt?   _____ No, I don't like bright colors.

   _____ Do you want a **b**erry red shirt?   _____ Yes, I want a strawberry-colored shirt.

2. _____ How many **b**oats do we need?   _____ Two. We can't all go fishing in one.

   _____ How many **v**otes do we need?   _____ Twenty, and we'll win the election.

3. _____ Did she park on the cur**b**?   _____ No! She parked on the sidewalk!

   _____ Did she park on the cur**ve**?   _____ No, she thought it was too dangerous.

4. _____ Did they pass the **b**an   _____ on smoking in restaurants?

   _____ Did they pass the **v**an   _____ on the left side of the road?

You and a group of your classmates must plan your dinner for this evening. The only problem is that you don't have much food in the house and you can't go to the store. With your classmates, plan a meal that you can all agree on, using only five foods from the lists below. Choose at least two foods from each list. Be sure to practice pronouncing /b/ and /v/ correctly.

Example:

A: Let's have broccoli for dinner.

B: I don't like broccoli. Can we have beets instead?

/b/	/v/
biscuits	**v**anilla ice cream
bread	**v**inegar
broccoli	salad with **v**inaigrette
black **b**eans	**v**egetables
beets	ra**v**ioli
ground **b**eef ham**b**urgers	**v**itamins
black**b**erries	**v**eal
bananas	a**v**ocados
bacon	oli**v**es

/b/ as in <u>b</u>ig, /p/ as in <u>p</u>ig, and /f/ as in <u>f</u>ight

All three of these sounds are made using the lips. /f/ also uses the top front teeth. To make /b/ sound different from /p/, you must make /b/ voiced and /p/ voiceless. For /f/, your top teeth must touch your bottom lip. When first practicing /f/, some students find it helpful to use their finger to hold the top lip away from the bottom lip until they can do it naturally.

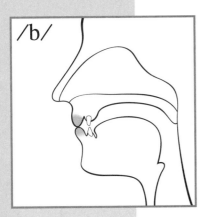

/b/

The top lip touches the bottom lip.
Air is completely stopped and then released.
/b/ is voiced.

Listen to examples of words with the /b/ sound: <u>b</u>ig, ha<u>b</u>it, la<u>b</u>

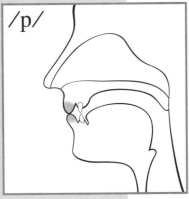

/p/

The top lip touches the bottom lip.
Air is completely stopped and then released.
/p/ is voiceless.

Hint: When /p/ is at the beginning of a word or a stressed syllable, you push out the air more strongly than when making a /p/ that is at the end of a syllable or that begins an unstressed syllable.

Listen to examples of words with the /p/ sound: <u>p</u>ig, ha<u>pp</u>y, to<u>p</u>

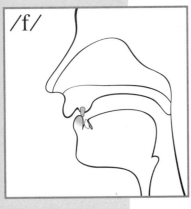

/f/

The top teeth are close to the bottom lip.
Air flows between the teeth and lip.
/f/ is voiceless.

Listen to examples of words with the /f/ sound: <u>f</u>ight, aw<u>f</u>ul, pu<u>ff</u>

Other spelling patterns: tele<u>ph</u>one, lau<u>gh</u>, hal<u>f</u>

A. Listen to this presentation on how the human heart works, and write in the words that are missing from the diagram. The first one is done for you.

Step 1: The blood needs to **(1)** _____*pick*_____ up more oxygen, so the heart pumps oxygen-
(2) _____ blood to the lungs to pick up oxygen from the air you **(3)** _____.

Step 4: The blood comes **(8)** _____ from the body and **(9)** _____ the heart again.

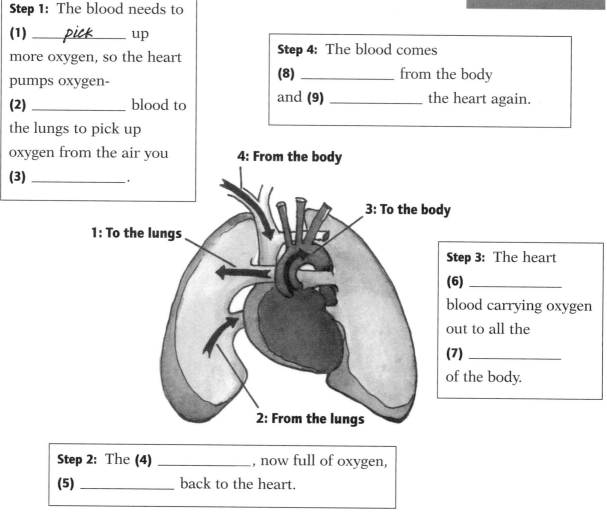

4: From the body

3: To the body

1: To the lungs

2: From the lungs

Step 3: The heart **(6)** _____ blood carrying oxygen out to all the **(7)** _____ of the body.

Step 2: The **(4)** _____, now full of oxygen, **(5)** _____ back to the heart.

Facts about your heart:
- Your heart is about the same size as your **(10)** _____.
- A person's pulse is about seventy-**(11)** _____ beats per minute.
- A baby's first heartbeats begin many months before it is **(12)** _____.

B. Listen to the first consonant sound in each word in these groups. Mark the word whose first consonant sound is different from the first consonant sound of the other two words. The first one is done for you.

1. _____   _____   __✗__

2. _____   _____   _____

3. _____   _____   _____

4. _____   _____   _____

5. _____   _____   _____

6. _____   _____   _____

Listen to the words again and repeat after the speaker. Be careful to pronounce the /b/, /p/, and /f/ sounds correctly.

Student A: Circle one of the two words in each sentence in the left column. Do not tell Student B which word you circled. Read the complete sentence to Student B.

Student B: Point to the picture that shows the meaning of the sentence Student A read.

After you and your partner have completed all the items, reverse roles and repeat the exercise.

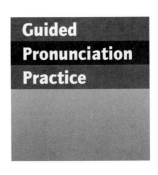
1. Did you like the **b**each / **p**each?

2. She took a **b**ath / **p**ath.

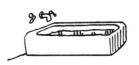 

3. He asked for a ro**b**e / ro**p**e.

4. She asked for a co**p**y / co**ff**ee.

5. They bought a new **p**an / **f**an.

6. Did he say **p**our / **f**our?

 4

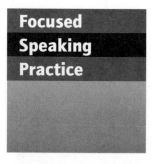
Read these symptoms of test anxiety, and mark your own feelings when you take a test. Then work with a partner to discuss a solution for at least three of these symptoms of test-taking anxiety. Share your suggestions with others in your class.

When you take a test, do you ever...	Always	Sometimes	Never
1. feel pain in your stomach or other parts of your body?	_____	_____	_____
2. have a very fast heartbeat, as if you were frightened?	_____	_____	_____
3. get sweaty hands and palms?	_____	_____	_____
4. skip class on the day of the test?	_____	_____	_____
5. feel that your mind is blank, and forget very simple things?	_____	_____	_____
6. worry that your pace is too slow when you see others finishing first?	_____	_____	_____
7. sleep poorly on the night before the test?	_____	_____	_____
8. think about tests you have failed in the past instead of focusing on doing your best?	_____	_____	_____
9. have difficulty following the directions on the test?	_____	_____	_____
10. think that you are dumb or feel sure that you will do badly on this test?	_____	_____	_____
11. forget the things that you studied, but remember the answers easily after the test is over?	_____	_____	_____
12. feel like you have to go to the bathroom because you're so nervous?	_____	_____	_____

Both of these sounds use the lips, but the /v/ sound also uses the bottom front teeth. Be careful to push air between the top teeth and bottom lip for /v/, but to push the lips out in front of the teeth for /w/.

/v/

The top teeth are close to the bottom lip.
Air flows between the teeth and lip.
/v/ is voiced.

Listen to examples of words with the /v/ sound: <u>v</u>an, e<u>v</u>er, mo<u>v</u>e

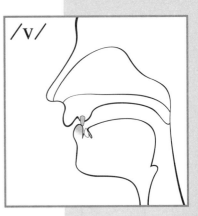

/w/

The back of the tongue is close to the roof of the mouth in the back.
The lips are rounded.
Air flows over the tongue and between the lips.
/w/ is voiced.

Listen to examples of words with the /w/ sound: <u>w</u>ait, <u>w</u>ould, a<u>w</u>ay

Other spelling patterns: <u>wh</u>ile*

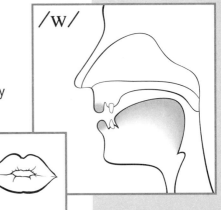

*In some dialects of English, words spelled with the letters *wh* are pronounced /hw/ and have an /h/ sound that comes before the /w/ sound.

A. Listen to this conversation between a driver and a police officer. The missing words have /v/ and /w/ sounds. Write in the missing words as you hear them. The first one is done for you.

Police Officer: Stay in your vehicle and **(1)** ___*wind*___ down the window. Give me your license and registration.

Driver: (2) _____ just a minute, please. Let me turn down the **(3)** _____ on my radio and get my license. It's in my **(4)** _____. Here you are. Was I doing anything wrong? Is this because I veered to the left back there?

Police Officer: Wait here while I **(5)** _____ that your license and registration are **(6)** _____.

Pause

Police Officer: (7) _____, then, Mr. Van Wick, what were you doing back there?

Driver: I thought I saw a child playing behind that white **(8)** _____. I was afraid she **(9)** _____ run out into the street. I was trying to **(10)** _____ an accident. That's why I turned the **(11)** _____ so quickly.

Police Officer: You were also driving **(12)** _____ quickly on these **(13)** _____ streets, and that is still a moving violation, but I'll let you off with a **(14)** _____ this time.

Driver: Thank you, officer.

Police Officer: In the future, though, you either **(15)** _____ more slowly or you **(16)** _____, you understand?

Driver: Yes, ma'am.

B. Listen to the first consonant sound in each word in these groups. Mark the word whose first consonant sound is different from the first consonant sound of the other two words. The first one is done for you.

1. __X__   _____   _____

2. _____   _____   _____

3. _____   _____   _____

4. _____   _____   _____

5. _____   _____   _____

6. _____   _____   _____

Listen to the words again and repeat after the speaker. Be careful to pronounce the /v/ and /w/ sounds correctly.

Student A: Put an X next to **one** phrase in each of the pairs in the left-hand column. Do not tell Student B which you marked. Read the phrase to Student B.

Student B: Listen to the phrase that Student A reads, and put an X next to the appropriate ending from the right-hand column.

After you and your partner have completed all four items, compare your answers. Then reverse roles and repeat the exercise.

1. _____ Did she say "**v**ow"?

   _____ Did she say "**w**ow"?

   _____ Yes, she's planning her wedding.

   _____ Yes. I guess she was surprised.

2. _____ Is that the **w**ine?

   _____ Is that the **v**ine?

   _____ No, I brought red wine, not white.

   _____ Yes, please cut it down.

3. _____ Did you leave your watch in the **v**est?

   _____ Did you leave your watch in the **w**est?

   _____ No, the pockets are empty.

   _____ Yes, I lost it there on vacation.

4. _____ Was the second book **w**orse?

   _____ Was the second book **v**erse?

   _____ No, I thought it was better than the first.

   _____ Yes, it was a book of poetry.

Read this story, and with a partner, create an ending to the story. Tell the story, including your ending, to a new partner. Be sure to pronounce /v/ and /w/ correctly.

1. **V**iolet **W**arner is a **w**ealthy **w**oman.

2. She called the police and said, "**V**ictor **W**illiams, who **w**orks for me, just robbed my house!"

3. The police inter**v**iewed two **w**itnesses.

4. **W**ally **V**an Dyke, a former friend o**f** **V**ictor's said, "**V**ictor is a **v**iolent man."

5. **V**anessa **W**ilcox, **V**iolet's neighbor, heard **V**ictor say "I'm **w**arning you, **V**iolet!"

6. The police got a **w**arrant, **v**isited **V**ictor's house, and arrested him.

7. In court, **V**iolet **W**arner told the judge that she **w**as a **v**ictim o**f** **V**ictor's **v**icious planning.

8. **V**ictor had a different **v**ersion o**f** the story.

9. His lawyer showed a **v**ideotape, **w**hich surprised e**v**eryone!

10. The **v**erdict **w**as "not guilty." **V**ictor **w**on!

What was **V**ictor's **v**ersion of the story? **Wh**at **w**as on the **v**ideotape?

/s/ as in sign and /z/ as in zero

These two sounds are both made by putting the tip of your tongue on your gum behind your teeth. /s/ is voiceless, and /z/ is voiced. It may help you practice if you put your hand on your throat to feel if you are voicing /z/.

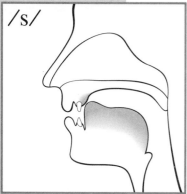

/s/

The tip of the tongue is close to the gum behind the top teeth.
Air flows between the tongue and the gum.
/s/ is voiceless.

Listen to examples of words with the /s/ sound: sing, nicer, boss

/z/

The tip of the tongue is close to the gum behind the top teeth.
Air flows between the tongue and the gum.
/z/ is voiced.

Listen to examples of words with the /z/ sound: zero, music, jazz

Hint: Voiceless /s/ sounds like a snake: *sssss* and voiced /z/ sounds like a bee: *zzzzz*.

A. Listen to this recorded telephone message about movies playing at different movie theaters. As you listen, fill in the blanks in the chart below with the title of the movie, the name of the theater where it can be seen, and the show times. The first one is done for you.

Movie Title	Cinema	Times
1. _Space Zombies_	Cinema Six	2. _____
Ice Eyes	3. _____	4. _____
5. _____	Spring Hill Mall	6. _____
7. _____	8. _____	6:30
It's a Zoo Out There	9. _____	10. _____
11. _____	12. _____	8:45

B. Listen to the pronunciation of these words. Place each word in the column for the sound it contains. The first one is done for you.

/s/ **as in sign**	/z/ **as in zero**
1. _____*six*_____	_____
2. _____	_____
3. _____	_____
4. _____	_____
5. _____	_____
6. _____	_____
7. _____	_____
8. _____	_____
9. _____	_____
10. _____	_____
11. _____	_____
12. _____	_____

Listen to the words again and repeat after the speaker. Pay attention to the /s/ and /z/ sounds.

Student A: Look at the chart below. Student B will work with the chart on page 158. Ask your partner questions to find out what each person does in his or her spare time. Your partner will ask you similar questions using the chart on page 158.

Guided Pronunciation Practice
Student A

Example:

Student A: What does Zoe do in her spare time?

Student B: Zoe does puzzles.

/z/	Zoe	Rose	Zachary	Liz
	does puzzles	______	goes to the zoo	______
/s/ and /z/	Suzy	Miss Zimmerman	Suzanne	Mr. Ziegler
	______	exercises	______	listens to jazz
/s/	Simon	Mr. Smith	Sally	Lisa
	skis	______	sings with her sister	______

Guided Pronunciation Practice
Student B

Student B: Look at the chart below. Student A will work with the chart on page 157. Ask your partner questions to find out what each person does in his or her spare time. Your partner will ask you similar questions using the chart on page 157.

Example:

Student A: What does Zoe do in her spare time?

Student B: Zoe does puzzles.

/z/	Zoe	Rose	Zachary	Liz
	does puzzles	plays music	______________	reads magazines
/s/ and /z/	Suzy	Miss Zimmerman	Suzanne	Mr. Ziegler
	visits museums	______________	socializes with friends	______________
/s/	Simon	Mr. Smith	Sally	Lisa
	______________	surfs the Internet	______________	dances

Work in a group of four. Each of you is responsible for one column in the chart below. Without telling your partners, choose one item from the column assigned to you. Write your choices and your partners' in the spaces below the chart. Then, with your partners, think of a story for the movie title, location, and movie stars you have each chosen. As you talk about the story, be sure to pronounce the /s/ and /z/ sounds correctly.

Example:

No Reason to Sing takes place in a large city and stars Catherine Zeta-Jones and Sylvester Stallone. The story is that Sylvester Stallone wants to be a famous singer, and he takes lessons from Catherine Zeta-Jones, who is a sad, unsuccessful rock musician.

Your movie can be a science fiction movie, a romance, a comedy, an action movie, a drama, a mystery, or anything your group chooses!

Student A: Choose a movie title.	Student B: Choose a setting for the movie.	Student C: Choose a female movie star.	Student D: Choose a male movie star.
Lazy Summer Days	A large city	Elizabeth Taylor	Bruce Willis
The Puzzle Murders	A zoo	Renee Zellweger	Tom Cruise
Quiz Zone	A jazz club	Susan Sarandon	Denzel Washington
No Reason to Sing	A small town	Cameron Diaz	Sylvester Stallone
The Rose Sisters	The desert	Catherine Zeta-Jones	Samuel L. Jackson

_____ takes place in _____ and stars
      (movie title)   **(location)**

_____ and _____ . The story is
      (female star)   **(male star)**

_____

_____

_____

_____

/s/ as in <u>s</u>ing, /ʃ/ as in <u>sh</u>op, and /tʃ/ as in <u>ch</u>eap

These sounds are all made by placing the tongue on the gum behind the top front teeth. However, /s/ uses the tip of the tongue, and the other two sounds use the middle of the tongue. For /ʃ/, just push air between the middle of the tongue and the gum; do not allow them to touch. For /tʃ/, touch the middle of the tongue to the gum and then force the air through.

/s/

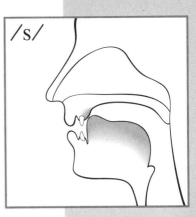

The tip of the tongue is close to the gum behind the top teeth.
Air flows between the tongue and the gum.
/s/ is voiceless.

Listen to examples of words with the /s/ sound: <u>s</u>ing, ni<u>c</u>er, bo<u>ss</u>

/ʃ/

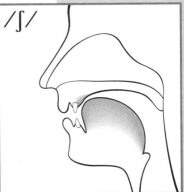

The middle of the tongue is close to the gum behind the top teeth.
Air flows between the tongue and the gum.
/ʃ/ is voiceless.

Listen to examples of words with the /ʃ/ sound: <u>sh</u>op, di<u>sh</u>es, wa<u>sh</u>

Other possible spellings: <u>su</u>re, mo<u>ti</u>on, so<u>ci</u>al

/tʃ/

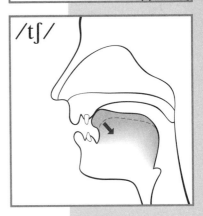

The middle of the tongue is close to the gum behind the top teeth.
Air is stopped and then pushed through the space between the tongue and the gum.
/tʃ/ is voiceless.

Listen to examples of words with the /tʃ/ sound: <u>ch</u>eap, bea<u>ch</u>es, ea<u>ch</u>

Other possible spellings: wa<u>tch</u>

A. Listen to this presentation about how a bill becomes a law. Write in the missing words as you hear them. The first one is done for you.

There are three different branches in the United States government. Each branch of the government has some powers; it also

(1) ___*checks*___ on the other branches to make sure that no one person or group becomes too powerful. This is called a

(2) _____ of checks and balances. Let's look at how this system of checks and balances works to (3) _____ a new law for the country.

Before a law is passed, it is called a bill. Bills start in Congress. In an election, U.S. citizens (4) _____ people to represent them in the two (5) _____ of Congress: the Senate and the House of Representatives. The bill can start in either chamber, but let's (6) _____ our bill starts in the Senate. First, the senators discuss the bill; then they vote. If more than half of the senators agree that the bill

(7) _____ be a law, it is sent to the House of Representatives for more discussion and another vote.

The U.S. President and the Supreme Court (8) _____ responsibility for making sure only good laws get passed in Congress. After both houses agree on a bill, the president must

(9) _____ it into law. Or, if the president wishes to

(10) _____ the bill from becoming law, he or she can veto it. This means the bill is (11) _____ back to Congress. Two-thirds of Congress must vote for the bill this time to cancel the president's veto. Finally, citizens can

(12) _____ a law in the Supreme Court. If the court

decides that the U.S. Constitution will not allow the law, it can

be **(13)** _____ or cancelled.

This is not a **(14)** _____ process, but it does help to

make **(15)** _____ that the laws of the country are fair.

B. Listen to the pronunciation of these words. Place each word in the column for the sound it contains. The first one is done for you.

/s/ as in sing	/ʃ/ as in shop	/tʃ/ as in change
1. _____	_____	_check_
2. _____	_____	_____
3. _____	_____	_____
4. _____	_____	_____
5. _____	_____	_____
6. _____	_____	_____
7. _____	_____	_____
8. _____	_____	_____
9. _____	_____	_____
10. _____	_____	_____
11. _____	_____	_____
12. _____	_____	_____
13. _____	_____	_____
14. _____	_____	_____
15. _____	_____	_____

Listen to these words again and repeat after the speaker. Be sure to pronounce the /s/, /ʃ/, and /tʃ/ sounds correctly.

Student A: You will work with this page. Student B will work with page 166. For each box below, circle one of the words or phrases. Dictate these sentences to Student B, who will write down the words you say in the blanks on page 166. Then reverse roles. The words in the Word Box will help you with spelling.

Word Box

charming
shrimp
munched on
chocolate chip
milkshake
cheesecake
ice cream sundae

I had a great time on

| **S**aturday |
| **S**unday |
| vaca**ti**on |

with my friends

| **S**teve |
| **Sh**erry |
| **Ch**arles |

and

| **Sh**elly |
| **S**ue |
| **Ch**ad |

. We

| wa**tch**ed a movie |
| **s**aw a **sh**ow |

and went shopping.

I

| **ch**ose |
| **s**elected |
| pur**ch**a**s**ed |

some

| ma**tch**ing |
| **ch**ecked |
| **sh**iny |

| **sh**oes |
| **sh**ort**s** |
| **sh**irt**s** |

.

Then we went to a _____ restaurant for _____,

where I had a delicious _____ _____. For

dessert we _____ a _____

_____.

For each item in the lists below, circle the one item you prefer. Tell a group of your classmates which item you chose and explain why. Be careful to pronounce the /s/, /ʃ/, and /tʃ/ sounds correctly.

Example:

A: I **ch**ose **c**innamon because it's a pretty brown color.

B: I **ch**ose **s**alt because I like **s**alty foods.

Which would you choose?

1. **s**ugar, **s**alt, **c**innamon

2. **ch**ef's salad, **ch**icken **s**oup, **ch**ili

3. ca**sh**, **ch**eck, **ch**arge

4. **c**elery, squa**sh**, spina**ch**

5. wa**sh**ing, poli**sh**ing, **s**weeping

6. **s**now, **s**un**sh**ine, **s**torms

7. wa**tch**, a **s**ilver bra**c**elet, a gold **ch**ain

8. a **s**pider, a **sh**ark, a cockroa**ch**

9. a **ch**air, a **s**ofa, a **s**tool

10. a ha**tch**back car, a four-door **s**edan, a **s**port**s** car

Student B: You will work with this page. Student A will work with page 164. Listen to Student A. In the blanks below, write down the words Student A says. Next, for each box, circle one of the words or phrases. Dictate these sentences to Student A, who will write down the words you say in the blanks on page 164. The words in the Word Box will help you with spelling.

I had a great time on _____ with my friends

_____ and _____. We _____

and went shopping. I _____ some _____

_____.

Word Box

Steve
Sherry
Charles
Shelly
Sue
Chad
watched a movie
saw a show

Then we went to a
| **ch**arming
cheap
cheerful |
restaurant for
| lun**ch**
supper
a **s**nack |
,

where I had a delicious
| fi**sh**
chicken
shrimp |
| **s**oup
salad
sandwi**ch** |
. For dessert

we
| **sh**ared
sampled
mun**ch**ed on |
a
| **s**trawberry
chocolate **ch**ip
cherry |
| milk**sh**ake
cheesecake
i**c**e cream **s**undae |
.

/tʃ/ as in <u>ch</u>eap, /dʒ/ as in <u>j</u>ob, and /y/ as in <u>y</u>ear

These three sounds are all made with the middle of the tongue. The difference between /tʃ/ and /dʒ/ is that /tʃ/ is voiceless and /dʒ/ is voiced. To make the /y/ sound, your tongue must be further back in the mouth than it is for the other two sounds.

/tʃ/

The middle of the tongue touches the gum behind the top teeth.
Air is stopped and then pushed through the space between the tongue and the gum.
/tʃ/ is voiceless.

Listen to examples of words with the /tʃ/ sound: <u>ch</u>eap, bea<u>ch</u>es, ea<u>ch</u>

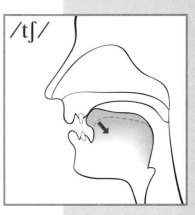

/dʒ/

The middle of the tongue touches the gum behind the top teeth.
Air is stopped and then pushed through the space between the tongue and the gum.
/dʒ/ is voiced.

Listen to examples of words with the /dʒ/ sound: <u>j</u>ob, <u>g</u>eneral, pa<u>g</u>es

Other spelling patterns: e<u>dg</u>e

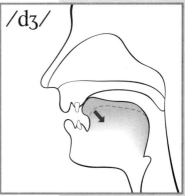

/y/

The middle of the tongue is close to the roof of the mouth.
Air flows between the tongue and the roof of the mouth.
/y/ is voiced.

Listen to examples of words with the /y/ sound: <u>y</u>ear, <u>y</u>es, <u>y</u>oung

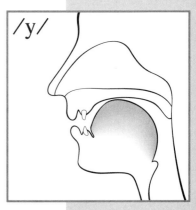

A. Listen to this presentation about the formation of the Himalayan Mountain range. Write in the missing words as you hear them. The first one is done for you.

The Himalayan Mountains are the tallest mountains in the world. The tallest mountain, Mt. Everest, is 8,854 meters high. How were these **(1)** ___*giant*___ mountains formed? Well, geologists believe that the Earth's surface is made of large **(2)** _____ of land called plates. These plates move, and their movement causes the Earth's surface to **(3)** _____. When the plates move quickly, they **(4)** _____ cause earthquakes. When they move slowly, they can form mountains like the Himalayas.

Two of these **(5)** _____ plates formed the Himalayas. These two plates are called the Indian plate and the Eurasian plate. The Indian plate started moving about 50 million **(6)** _____ ago. It jammed into the Eurasian plate with **(7)** _____ force that it pushed a large piece of the Eurasian plate up into a ridge. **(8)** _____ your book if you want to see a **(9)** _____ showing how this happened.

That ridge grew into the Himalayan Mountains, and most of that growth happened **(10)** _____ in the last 10 million years. Ten million years seems like a long time, but in fact, that is a very **(11)** _____ age for mountains. These tall mountains may grow taller **(12)** _____. Geologists have

been **(13)** _____ the growth of the Himalayas, and their

research shows that these mountains are still growing about

one centimeter **(14)** _____.

EURASIAN PLATE

INDIA
Today

10 million
years ago

38 million
years ago

55 million
years ago

71 million
years ago

"INDIA"
Land mass

SRI LANKA

INDIAN
OCEAN

SRI LANKA

B. Listen to the consonant sounds in these pairs of words. Some pairs start with the same consonant sound and some start with different consonant sounds. Circle *same* or *different* to show which you hear. The first one is done for you.

1. same   ⟨different⟩

2. same   different

3. same   different

4. same   different

5. same   different

6. same   different

7. same   different

8. same   different

For the next two pairs, listen to the consonants at the ends of the words. Are they the same or different?

9. same   different

10. same   different

Listen to the words again and repeat after the speaker. Be careful to pronounce the /tʃ/, /dʒ/, and /y/ sounds correctly.

Student A: Put an X next to **one** phrase in each of the pairs in the left-hand column. Do not tell Student B which you marked. Read the phrase to Student B.

Student B: Listen to the phrase that Student A reads, and put an X next to the appropriate ending from the right-hand column.

After you and your partner have completed all six items, compare your answers. Then reverse roles and repeat the exercise.

1. _____ Do you have a ma**tch**?   _____ I want to light a candle.
   _____ Do you have a Ma**dge**   _____ in your class? I'm looking for her.

2. _____ Have you seen Mar**ch**'s report? _____ I have April's but not March's.
   _____ Have you seen Mar**ge**'s report? _____ It's more than 30 pages long!

3. _____ Did you buy a **ch**eap   _____ stereo or an expensive one?
   _____ Did you buy a **J**eep   _____ Cherokee or some other kind of car?

4. _____ He went to **Y**ale because he was _____ a good student.
   _____ He went to **j**ail because he was _____ a criminal.

5. _____ It was **J**ello,   _____ not pudding.
   _____ It was **y**ellow,   _____ not green.

6. _____ She took the **y**olk   _____ of the egg out of the bowl.
   _____ She took the **j**oke   _____ well and didn't get offended.

You work for an International Spy Agency. It is your job to create secret identities for the spies. To create a secret identity, circle one answer in each of the rows below. Then you and your classmates will try to guess the identities of each other's spies. Ask a partner yes and no questions to try to learn which answers your partner has circled. When you have correctly learned each other's answers, find new partners, and do the activity again.

Example:

A: Is your spy's name **Ch**arles?

B: No. Does your spy usually wear a **j**ean **j**acket?

A: **Y**es.

	/tʃ/	/y/	/dʒ/
Name	**Ch**arles	**Y**olanda	**J**amie
Favorite food	**ch**ocolate **ch**ip cookies	**y**ogurt	**j**elly sandwiches
Enjoys	playing **ch**ess	practicing **y**oga	listening to **j**azz
Usually wears	a **ch**eap gold wa**tch**	the color **y**ellow	a **j**ean **j**acket
People say s/he...	is **ch**eerful.	looks **y**oung for his/her age.	tells good **j**okes.

/n/ as in n̲ice and /l/ as in l̲ight

These two sounds are made by placing the tongue in the same place: on the gum behind the top front teeth. The difference is that /n/ is a nasal sound. That means the air comes through the nose, not the mouth.

/n/

The tip of the tongue touches the gum behind the top teeth.
Air is stopped and flows through the nose.
/n/ is voiced.

Listen to examples of words with the /n/ sound: n̲ice, wi̲n̲n̲er, pe̲n̲

Other spelling patterns: kn̲ee, pn̲eumonia, si̲g̲n̲

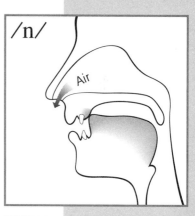

/l/

The tip of the tongue touches the gum behind the top teeth.
Air flows around the side of the tongue.
/l/ is voiced.

Listen to examples of words with the /l/ sound: l̲ight, si̲l̲ly, mi̲l̲e

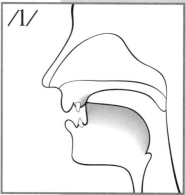

A. Listen to these people talk about their favorite holiday traditions. Write in the missing words as you hear them. The first one is done for you.

A: Halloween is always a **(1)** _____fun_____ holiday. Children wear costumes and **(2)** _____ on doors and say "trick or treat." We don't **(3)** _____ our doors on Halloween because we'll open them many times. Every child goes home with a **(4)** _____ bag of candy.

B: It's always great **(5)** _____ when my favorite college team plays football in a bowl game on New Year's Day. My whole family watches on TV and cheers for our team so they **(6)** _____ **(7)** _____. Our family joke is that if we cheer loudly enough, the team can't **(8)** _____.

C: On Christmas Eve, our children try to stay

up all **(9)** _____. They think every

(10) _____ they see in the sky is Santa

Claus. But they always fall asleep before the

(11) _____ of presents appears under

our decorated **(12)** _____ tree.

D: Every year on Thanksgiving we have a big **(13)** _____.

My father takes a big **(14)** _____ and carves a piece of

turkey for each of us, but **(15)** _____ until after my

mother **(16)** _____ us in remembering the many things

we are thankful for in **(17)** _____ and how our

(18) _____ have been met

this year. This holiday really

(19) _____ a

(20) _____ to me.

B. Listen to this list of words. Circle the word that you hear. The first one is done for you.

1. (fun)   full

2. knock   lock

3. news   lose

4. will   win

5. night   light

6. pine   pile

7. mean   meal

8. knife   life

9. needs   leads

10. not   lot

Listen to the words again and repeat after the speaker. Be careful to pronounce the /n/ and /l/ sounds correctly.

Student A: Put an X next to **one** phrase in each of the pairs in the left-hand column. Do not tell Student B which you marked. Read the phrase to Student B.

Student B: Listen to the phrase that Student A reads, and put an X next to the appropriate ending from the right-hand column.

After you and your partner have completed all four items, compare your answers. Then reverse roles and repeat the exercise.

1. _____ The project is du**ll**.   _____ Can we make it more interesting?

   _____ The project is do**ne**.   _____ Now we can go home and relax.

2. _____ There is a **n**ine   _____ in my phone number.

   _____ There is a **l**ine   _____ outside the store because of the
                                                    sale.

3. _____ There were **n**o clouds in the sky,   _____ and it was very sunny.

   _____ There were **l**ow clouds in the sky   _____ before it started to rain.

4. _____ I tied a **kn**ot   _____ in my shoelace and can't untie it.

   _____ I tied a **l**ot   _____ of shoes when I worked in a shoe
                                                    store.

A compound word is formed by combining two or more smaller words. For example, *sunglasses* is a compound words made up of the words *sun* and *glasses*. The words *life*, *light*, *love*, *knee*, *news*, and *night* combine with many words to form compounds.

Work with a group of classmates to make at least three compound words using each of these words. You may use words from the Word Box. Can you make more than three with any of these words? Be sure to pronounce the /n/ and /l/ sounds correctly. Check a dictionary if you need help.

Word Box

birds
bulb
cap
club
deep
flash
group
high
house
letter
like
line
long
paper
school
show
sick
sock
stand
time
weight
year

1. life _____

2. life _____

3. life _____

4. knee _____

5. knee _____

6. knee _____

7. love _____

8. love _____

9. love _____

10. night _____

11. night _____

12. night _____

13. light _____

14. light _____

15. light _____

16. news _____

17. news _____

18. news _____

/m/ as in <u>m</u>ap, /n/ as in <u>n</u>ice, and /ŋ/ as in bri<u>ng</u>

The sounds /m/, /n/, and /ŋ/ are *nasal* sounds. These sounds are made by pushing air through your nose instead of your mouth. To do this, you will have to lower your soft palate to shut the passage from your throat to your mouth.

/m/

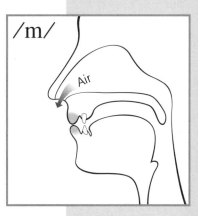

The top lip touches the bottom lip.
Air is stopped and flows through the nose.
/m/ is voiced.

Listen to examples of words with the /m/ sound: <u>m</u>ap, su<u>mm</u>er, hi<u>m</u>

Other spelling patterns: cli<u>mb</u>, ca<u>lm</u>, hy<u>mn</u>

/n/

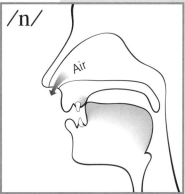

The tip of the tongue touches the gum behind the top teeth.
Air is stopped and flows through the nose.
/n/ is voiced.

Listen to examples of words with the /n/ sound: <u>n</u>ice, wi<u>nn</u>er, pe<u>n</u>

Other spelling patterns: <u>kn</u>ee, <u>pn</u>eumonia, si<u>gn</u>

/ŋ/

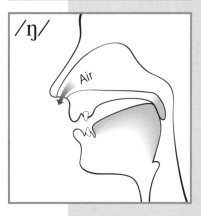

The back of the tongue touches the back of the roof of the mouth.
Air is stopped and then flows through the nose.
/ŋ/ is voiced.

Listen to examples of words with the /ŋ/ sound: bri<u>ng</u>, so<u>ng</u>, a<u>ng</u>ry, stre<u>ng</u>th, ba<u>n</u>k

Hint: In English, this sound cannot come at the beginning of syllables.

A. Listen to this list of words. Circle the word that you hear. The first one is done for you.

1. some   (sun)   6. bam   bang

2. moon   noon   7. thing   thin

3. wrong   Ron   8. think   thick

4. rang   ran   9. came   cane

5. teams   teens   10. mine   nine

B. You will hear each of the following sentences twice. Write in the missing words as you hear them. Pay careful attention to the /m/, /n/, and /ŋ/ sounds at the ends of the missing words. The first one is done for you.

1. They went out to get ___*some*___ _____.

2. I _____ the soup is too _____.

3. All the players on those _____ are _____.

4. Did it sound like a " _____ " or a " _____ "?

5. Those _____ are _____.

6. The man with the _____ _____ yesterday.

7. _____ is almost never _____.

8. Have you seen the _____ at _____?

9. They _____ the doorbell then _____ away.

10. I forgot that this _____ was so _____.

Listen to the sentences again and repeat after the speaker. Be careful to pronounce the /m/, /n/, and /ŋ/ sounds correctly.

Student A: You will work with this page. Student B will work with page 182. For each box below, circle one of the words or phrases. Dictate these sentences to Student B, who will write down the words you say in the blanks on page 182. Then reverse roles. The words in the Word Box will help you with spelling.

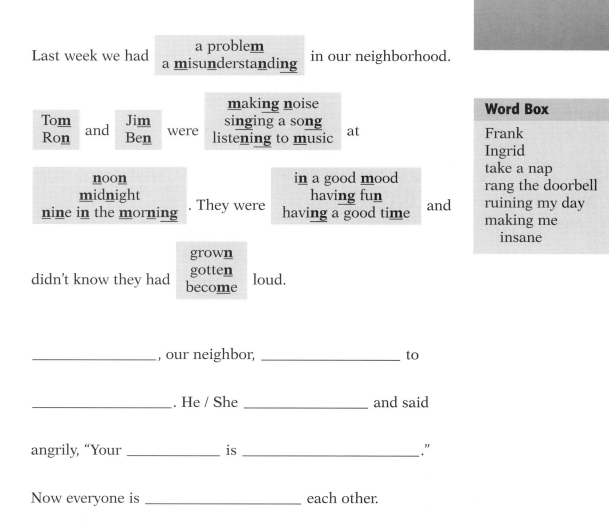

Last week we had [a proble**m** / a **mi**su**n**dersta**n**di**ng**] in our neighborhood.

[To**m** / Ro**n**] and [Jim / Be**n**] were [**m**aki**ng n**oise / si**ng**ing a so**ng** / liste**n**ing to **m**usic] at

[**n**oon / **mi**d**n**ight / **ni**ne **in** the **mor**ning] . They were [**in** a good **m**ood / havi**ng** fu**n** / havi**ng** a good ti**m**e] and

didn't know they had [grow**n** / gotte**n** / beco**m**e] loud.

Word Box

Frank
Ingrid
take a nap
rang the doorbell
ruining my day
making me
    insane

_____ , our neighbor, _____ to

_____ . He / She _____ and said

angrily, "Your _____ is _____ ."

Now everyone is _____ each other.

Student B: You will work with this page. Student A will work with page 181. Listen to Student A. In the blanks below, write down the words Student A says. Next, for each box, circle one of the two words or phrases. Dictate these sentences to Student A, who will write down the words you say in the blanks on page 181. The words in the Word Box will help you with spelling.

Last week we had a _____ in our neighborhood.

_____ and _____ were _____

at _____. They were _____

and didn't know they had _____ loud.

Word Box

misunderstanding
Tom
Ron
Jim
Ben
in a good mood

| Frank Ingrid | , our neighbor, | was trying
needed | to | take a **n**ap
watch a ga**m**e
get so**m**e rest | . |

He / She | ra**ng** the doorbell
pho**n**ed their ho**m**e
knocked o**n** their door | and said angrily,

"Your | **n**oise
music
shouti**ng** | is | rui**n**i**ng m**y day
maki**ng m**e in**s**a**n**e
not very **n**ice | ." Now everyone

is | **m**ad at
a**ng**ry with
not talki**ng** to | each other.

Complete the chart below with something you *were doing* in the past time periods shown and with something you think you *will be doing* in the future time periods shown. Work with a partner and compare your activities, then report your results to others in your class. As you report, be sure to pronounce the /m/, /n/, and /ŋ/ sounds correctly.

Example:

> In 1999, I was living with my grandmother, and Hong was learning to play the guitar.

Past time periods	You	Your Partner
Nineteen Ninety Nine (1999)	_____	_____
	_____	_____
One year ago	_____	_____
	_____	_____
Last month	_____	_____
	_____	_____
Future time periods		
Next month	_____	_____
	_____	_____
In one year	_____	_____
	_____	_____
Ten years from now	_____	_____
	_____	_____

When you make the /h/ sound correctly your vocal cords will not vibrate, but you can feel a slight tightness in your throat. You make a similar sound when you laugh or breathe heavily.

/h/

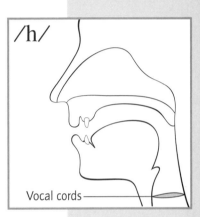

The vocal cords are tight, but they do not vibrate.
Air flows through the vocal cords.
/h/ is voiceless.

Listen to examples of words that start with the /h/ sound: have, high, how

Hint: Be careful not to confuse words that begin with /h/ with similar sounding words that do not start with an /h/ sound.

Examples:

hungry	angry
hair	air

Also be careful not to confuse /h/ and /f/.

Examples:

harm	farm
heat	feet

A. Listen to this conversation between a nurse and her patient. Look at the form the nurse is completing, and fill in the missing words.

Patient Information Form

Name: _Oscar Mehta_

Address: _1456 Aliso Way, Apt. 45, Houston, TX_

Phone: _281-555-6786_

(1) ___Height___ : _5 ft. 10 in._ Weight: _185_

Blood pressure: _119/85_

(2) _____ rate: _79_

A. Have there been any changes to your **(3)** _____

(4) _____ since your last visit?

Yes (No)

B. Have you had any surgery or **(5)** _____ stays since your last visit?

Yes (No)

C. Do you have any **(6)** _____ that could be

(7) _____ to your health?

None (Smoking) Alcohol Drugs Other

Notes: _The patient is trying to quit._

D. What medical **(8)** _____ do you need today?

Notes: _The patient says he_ **(9)** _____ _down in the_

(10) _____ _yesterday at his_ **(11)** _____ . _He hurt his foot and his_ **(12)** _____ .

B. Listen to the first sounds in these pairs of words. Some pairs have the same sound and some have different sounds. Circle *same* or *different* to show which you hear. The first one is done for you.

1. same   (different)

2. same   different

3. same   different

4. same   different

5. same   different

6. same   different

7. same   different

8. same   different

9. same   different

10. same   different

Listen to the words again, and repeat after the speaker. Be careful to pronounce the /h/ sounds correctly.

Student A: Put an X next to **one** phrase in each of the pairs in the left-hand column. Do not tell Student B which you marked. Read the phrase to Student B.

Student B: Listen to the phrase that Student A reads, and put an X next to the appropriate ending from the right-hand column.

After you and your partner have completed all five items, compare your answers. Then reverse roles and repeat the exercise.

1. _____ She's lost her **h**earing.   _____ She must wear a hearing aid.

   _____ She's lost her earring.   _____ It fell out of her ear.

2. _____ He gave her his **h**eart.   _____ And she broke it.

   _____ He gave her his art.   _____ She hung it on the wall.

3. _____ I can feel the **h**air.   _____ It's tickling the back of my neck.

   _____ I can feel the air.   _____ It's blowing through the window.

4. _____ We met in the fall,   _____ in October to be exact.

   _____ We met in the **h**all   _____ after classes were over.

5. _____ There is nothing to **h**ear.   _____ Everything is silent.

   _____ There is nothing to fear.   _____ Be brave!

Interview your classmates to find out if they have *often*, *sometimes*, or *never* done each of the things in the chart below. Add an item of your choice in the last space on the chart. Try to use words that begin with /h/.

Use phrases like "Did you ever...?" and "Do you ever...?"

	Name	Name	Name
Host parties at home			
Have long hair			
Ride on a horse			
Break a bad habit			
Have to stay in a hospital			
Have a broken heart			
Help paint a house			

Putting Sounds Together

The things you will learn in this part can help you to improve your listening comprehension. Dictations from recordings are one good way to check your listening comprehension. Listen to short recordings of English speech, pause the recording after each phrase, and write down what you think you hear. You will have to listen carefully. After you have written everything as accurately as you can, check your dictation by asking someone else to listen and read your dictation for errors, or, if you can, check a script of the recording. The mistakes you make will help you to see where you can improve your listening comprehension. If you would like to try, there are several practice dictations on the Sound Bites website.

When you are trying to learn a new sound, it is a good idea to practice making the sound alone and in short words. However, when people speak, they move their tongues and mouths very quickly, and sometimes the sounds are changed by the sounds around them. In Part Five, you will learn about some of the difficulties that students of English have when they put sounds together. It is a good idea to study these chapters after you have practiced most of the consonants and vowels that are difficult for you. You may be surprised at some of the changes that happen when people use sounds and words in fast speech!

Chapter 36

Final Consonants

In American English, the last consonant in a word is often not released. This means that after you say the last consonant sound, you keep the parts of your mouth that make the sound closed. If you release the consonant sound by opening your mouth, your listener may think that you have added an extra syllable to the word you are saying.

Listen to examples of words with non-released and released final consonants.

Unreleased:	Released (sounds like):
hel**p**	hel**p a**
sew**ed**	so**da**
Me**g**	me**ga**

These sounds are unreleased:

/p/, /b/, /t/, /d/, /k/, /g/, /ð/, /v/, /z/

Be sure that you don't add an /iy/ sound after these sounds:

/ʃ/, /tʃ/ /dʒ/, and /ʒ/.

For example, say

Engli**sh** (not Englishy)

bea**ch** (not beachy)

langua**ge** (not languagey)

gara**ge** (not garagey)

When you practice these final consonants, be sure that you don't allow them to disappear completely.

Listen to examples of words that do not end in a consonant and words that do end in a consonant:

May does not end in a consonant, but ma**ke** does.

Be does not end in a consonant, but bea**ch** does.

Why does not end in a consonant, but wi**de** and whi**te** do.

See Chapter 37 for more information on final consonants and their effect on vowel length.

A. Circle *yes* if you hear a final consonant and *no* if you do not. The first one is done for you.

1. yes   (no)

2. yes   no

3. yes   no

4. yes   no

5. yes   no

6. yes   no

7. yes   no

8. yes   no

9. yes   no

10. yes   no

B. In each of these sentence pairs, the underlined word in the first sentence has an unreleased final consonant. In the second sentence, the underlined word has an unreleased final consonant, but it sounds as though it is released because it is linked to the reduced vowel that follows it. Mark the sentence that you hear. The first one is done for you.

1. __X__ a. Sing **it** loud.

_____ b. Sing **it** aloud.

2. _____ a. Make sure you **keep** count

_____ b. Make sure you **keep** a count.

3. _____ a. He **spoke** while they listened.

_____ b. He **spoke** awhile; they listened.

4. _____ a. **She's** voiding it now.

_____ b. **She's** avoiding it now.

5. _____ a. Is the **globe** round?

_____ b. Is the **globe** around?

6. _____ a. Is **Meg** head of it?

_____ b. Is **Meg** ahead of it?

7. _____ a. Did you **finish** mailing it?

_____ b. Did you **finish** e-mailing it?

8. _____ a. They **change** motions quickly.

_____ b. They **change** emotions quickly.

9. _____ a. I got the **watch** specially for you.

_____ b. I got the **watch** especially for you.

10. _____ a. There was nothing he **could** prove.

_____ b. There was nothing he **could** approve.

Listen again, and repeat the sentences after the speaker. Be careful to pronounce the final consonants correctly.

Guided Pronunciation Practice
Student A

A riddle is a question with an unexpected or a silly answer.

Look at the chart below. Student B will work with the chart on page 196.

Take turns reading the riddles on your page to your partner, and choose the answers to your partner's riddles. Be sure to pronounce the final consonants in the underlined words correctly.

Student A Riddles
1. What is the favorite dessert of a ghost?
2. Where do you put your dog while you shop?
3. What is the saddest day of the week?
4. Why do lions eat raw meat?

Answers
1. A kitten.
2. Silence.
3. It's two tired. (too tired)
4. Black and white and read all over. (red)

Guided Pronunciation Practice Student B

A riddle is a question with an unexpected or a silly answer.

Look at the chart below. Student A will work with the chart on page 195.

Take turns reading the riddles on your page to your partner, and choose the answers to your partner's riddles. Be sure to pronounce the final consonants in the underlined words correctly.

Student B Answers
A. In a barking lot.
B. Sadder day. (Saturday)
C. Ice cream. (I scream)
D. They never learned to cook.
Riddles
A. What can you break with one word?
B. Why won't a bike stand up by itself?
C. What color is a newspaper?
D. What has a head and tail like a cat but isn't a cat?

Choose at least five of the "answers" below, and work with a group of classmates to make up questions that could have these answers. Be sure to pronounce the final consonants correctly.

Example:

> If the answer is "a hot dog," the question could be "What is my pet in the summer?" or "What did I have for lunch?" or "What kind of food does Nori hate the most?"

Answers

a picku**p** tru**ck**	a re**d** ro**se** bu**d**	ba**d** foo**d**
a heada**che**	birthday ca**ke**	a ca**b** ri**de**
the glo**be**	a bi**g** fro**g**	the Engli**sh** langua**ge**
nex**t** wee**k**	a qui**ck** sna**ck**	the perfec**t** a**ge**

Voiced and voiceless consonants can change the vowel sounds in front of them. When a vowel is followed by a voiced consonant, make it longer. When a vowel is followed by a voiceless consonant, make it shorter. It should take you a little longer to say a word that ends in a voiced consonant than it takes you to say a word ending in a voiceless consonant.

Listen to the examples. First, you will hear a word that ends in a voiced consonant and has a lengthened vowel sound. Next you will hear a similar word that ends in a voiceless consonant and has a shortened vowel sound.

Lengthened Vowel	Shortened Vowel
bad	bat
robe	rope
save	safe
ridge	rich
raise	race
bag	back

A. Listen and circle the word you hear. Then decide whether that word ends in a voiced consonant and has a lengthened vowel sound or whether it ends in a voiceless consonant and has a shortened vowel sound. The first one is done for you.

		Voiced consonant, lengthened vowel	Voiceless consonant, shortened vowel
1. rag	(rack)	_____	___X___
2. rib	rip	_____	_____
3. feed	feet	_____	_____
4. prove	proof	_____	_____
5. ridge	rich	_____	_____
6. lose	loose	_____	_____
7. peas	peace	_____	_____
8. said	set	_____	_____

B. Listen to these sentences, and circle the picture that illustrates the sentence that you hear. The first one is done for you.

1. It's in the bag / back.

2. He hit / hid it.

3. We saw his knees / niece.

4. There's a cap / cab over there.

5. I found a buck / bug.

6. They're going to leave / leaf.

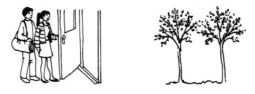

Listen to the sentences again and repeat after the speaker. Pay attention to the pronunciation of vowel length.

We say that two words rhyme when they have the same ending sounds. Often, this means that the words share a vowel sound and consonant sound at the end, like *long* and *wrong* or *days* and *raise*. Notice that sometimes the spelling is different, but the sounds are the same.

Fill in the word from the box that rhymes with the underlined word in each sentence. Your teacher may ask you to work with a partner. Pay attention to the vowel sounds that come before voiced and voiceless consonant endings. The first one is done for you.

1. To win the **race**, keep up the _____*pace*_____.

2. If you want a **raise**, see the one who _____.

3. Those beautiful **eyes** can tell no _____.

4. This drink is **nice** when drunk with _____.

5. The cat in her **lap** was taking a _____.

6. She saw a frog on a **slab** when she entered the _____.

7. That's my friend **Madge** who's wearing the _____.

8. It's a great **match** from the same _____.

9. When you get **back**, we'll have a _____.

10. There was an old **rag** in the bottom of the _____.

11. We felt a lot of **grief** when we heard he was a _____.

12. I couldn't **believe** he was planning to _____.

13. That's the **note** she said that she _____.

14. The truck had to **unload** in the middle of the _____.

15. He took his favorite **robe** on his trip around the _____.

16. I really do **hope** you bought some _____.

Word Box
badge
bag
batch
globe
ice
lab
leave
lies
nap
pace
pays
road
snack
soap
thief
wrote

Write a plus (+) above the rhyming words that end in voiced consonants and write a minus (−) above the words that end in voiceless consonants. Practice reading the sentences. Be sure to make the words with + signs longer than the words with − signs.

Add three verbs to each list of past tense verbs. The words in the first list should have voiceless consonants after the vowel, and the verbs in the second list should have voiced consonants after the vowel. Then make up a story using as many verbs from the two lists as possible. Be sure to lengthen or shorten the vowels and to pronounce the vowels correctly.

Past verbs with voiceless consonants after the vowel (shortened vowel sound)	Past verbs with voiced consonants after the vowel (lengthened vowel sound)
me**t**	so**l**d
too**k**	ga**v**e
lo**st**	hi**d**
wa**sh**ed	hea**r**d
hi**t**	fou**n**d
wa**tch**ed	gra**bb**ed
sto**pp**ed	hu**gg**ed
lau**gh**ed	wa**v**ed
_____	_____
_____	_____
_____	_____
_____	_____

_____

_____

_____

_____

_____

_____

In most dialects of North American English, these two simple English words — *can* and *can't* — are sometimes very difficult to understand when they are spoken in a sentence. This is because the rules of pronunciation and sentence stress cause these words to sound different when they are pronounced in a sentence and when they are pronounced alone.

Can't is usually pronounced /kæn/ because it is a stressed word with a full vowel and a reduced /t/. (See Chapter 45 for more information on reduced /t/.)

Can is pronounced /kən/ because it is an unstressed word with a reduced vowel. (See Chapter 5 to review reduced vowels.)

Listen to the examples:

> We **can** do that.

> We **can't** do that.

This means that *can't* often sounds like *can*. As a result of its reduced vowel, *can* usually sounds something like *kun*. No wonder it is confusing! Even native speakers get confused. Sometimes the grammar of the sentence can help you figure out whether a person said *can* or *can't*. And you can always ask, "Did you say *can* or *cannot*?"

Listen to this conversation about studying for the written part of the driver's license test. Pay special attention to the use of *can* and *can't*. Then listen to sentences from the conversation and decide whether the speaker says *can* or *can't*. Circle the word you hear. The first one is done for you.

1. I'm studying for my driving test —(Can)/ can't you quiz me?

2. Give me the manual so you can / can't cheat!

3. How close can / can't you park to a fire hydrant?

4. I can / can't remember.

5. How close to a hydrant can't / can you park?

6. I'll bet you can / can't answer this one.

7. When can / can't you pass another car?

8. You can / can't pass when there's a double yellow line on the road.

9. I can / can't believe it! That's right!

10. Maybe you can / can't pass this test after all.

Listen again and repeat the sentences after the speaker. Pay attention to the pronunciation of *can* and *can't*.

Read each of the statements below. Circle *can* or *can't* to make the statement true for yourself. Then add at least two statements of your own. Read the statements about yourself to a group of classmates. Your classmates will nod their heads *yes* if you say *can*, and will shake their heads *no* if you say *can't*. This will help you to check your pronunciation of *can* and *can't*.

Guided Pronunciation Practice

1. I can / can't speak three languages.

2. I can / can't sing well.

3. I can / can't run a marathon.

4. I can / can't drive a car.

5. I can / can't swim.

6. I can / can't bake a cake.

7. I can / can't play tennis.

8. _____

9. _____

10. _____

Look at these traffic signs, and with a small group of your classmates, discuss what each sign means. Use *can't* and *can* in your discussion, and be careful to pronounce both words correctly. *Hint:* First say what the sign says you **can't** do.

Example:

A: That's a stop sign. It means that you **can't** go forward until after you stop.

B: That's right. After you stop and look both ways, you **can** go.

In spoken English, words are often connected, or *linked*, together. Linking sounds appropriately can help your speech to sound smooth and fluent. There are several types of sounds that can be linked together. In this chapter, you will study two kinds of linking.

When a word ending in a consonant is followed by a word starting in a vowel, link the consonant to the vowel.

Listen to the examples:

lived in   help us   find out

When a word ending in a consonant is followed by a word beginning with the same consonant, link these words together, and say the sound only once.

Listen to the examples:

short time   feel like   has something

Remember, linking is based on sounds, not spelling. So "clear writing" is linked, but "comb back" is not.

For information about more kinds of linking, see the *Sound Bites* website.

A. In the following sentences, circle the sounds that you think will be linked. You may work with a partner. Then, listen to the sentences to check your predictions. The first one is done for you.

1. I feel like singing.

2. We finished it in no time.

3. I have lots of ideas, but I lack cash.

4. Stop putting your books on the table.

5. Did you bring both things I asked for?

6. You went around that curve very fast.

7. It's important to watch children carefully.

8. There's a deep pool behind our house.

Listen to the sentences again, and repeat them after the speaker. Be careful to link the words as the speaker on the recording does.

B. Listen to these sentences three times. Listen first to understand the meaning. The second time you listen, fill in the missing words. The missing words are linked, so listen carefully to be sure that you understand them correctly. The third time you listen, check your work.

1. Sometimes ___*students*___ ___*are*___ ___*unhappy*___ that they must study chemistry.

2. They may not realize that chemistry is _____ _____ day _____ _____ lives.

3. Chemicals _____ _____ _____ _____ baking soda are used a _____ _____ for cooking.

4. Do you ever _____ _____ or tea without caffeine?

5. Three _____ _____ _____ chemical reactions can make decaffeinated coffee.

6. Are you interested in your _____ _____ beauty? _____ _____ require chemistry.

7. When you _____ _____, you are clean _____ _____ the chemistry of soap.

8. If fluoride _____ _____ antacids _____ _____ your bathroom, you make _____ _____ chemistry.

9. Chemists even know why _____ _____ be one color in the tube and _____ _____ brighter on someone's lips.

10. So, _____ _____ think they don't _____ _____, but, in fact, they use it every day.

C. Notice how the words you have written are linked. Can you find any other words that were linked in the sentences? Circle any additional linked words. (There are at least ten additional examples of linking.)

These three poems are the lyrics to songs that children often learn to sing in clubs and at camps. Several examples of linking are marked in each poem. Read the poems to a partner. Your partner will listen carefully to hear if you using linking correctly.

Poem 1

Make new friends but keep the old,

O**ne is s**ilve**r a**nd the other gold.

A circle's round, it has no end,

That's how long I wan**t t**o be your friend.

I ha**ve a** hand, and you ha**ve a**nother,

Put them togethe**r a**nd we ha**ve each o**ther.

Poem 2

Somewhere there**'s a** forest

Where you can stan**d and d**ream

And wal**k a**lone beside the waters

O**f a** fore**st st**ream

Poem 3

Lo**ve is s**omethi**ng if** you gi**ve it a**way,

Gi**ve it a**way, gi**ve it a**way.

Lo**ve is s**omethi**ng if** you gi**ve it a**way;

You en**d u**p having more.

It's just li**ke a** magic penny;

Hol**d it t**ight, and you won't ha**ve a**ny;

Len**d i**t, spen**d i**t, and you'll have so many

They'll ro**ll all o**ver the floor.

—Malvina Reynold

The following sentences are unfinished. Add one or more words that can link with the last word of each unfinished sentence. You can use a word that begins with a vowel, or a word that begins with the consonant sound at the end of the unfinished sentence. Say your sentences to a partner. Remember to use linking.

1. I want to have _____

   _____ .

2. It was a small _____

   _____ .

3. When the movie ended _____

   _____ .

4. They'll do it again _____

   _____ .

5. Is that the right _____

   _____ ?

6. After they got back _____

   _____ .

7. My friend and I both _____

   _____ .

8. You have to stop _____

   _____ .

Chapter 40

The difference between numbers ending in *-teen* (like 14, 16, and 19) and numbers ending in *-ty* (like 40, 60, and 90) is mostly a difference in syllable stress.

For numbers ending in *-teen*, stress the last syllable:
thir**TEEN**, fif**TEEN**.

For numbers ending in *-ty*, stress the first syllable, not the *-ty* syllable:
THIRty, **FIF**ty.

Listen to the examples:

thir **TEEN**	**THIR** ty
four **TEEN**	**FOR** ty
fif **TEEN**	**FIF** ty
six **TEEN**	**SIX** ty
seven **TEEN**	**SEV** en ty
eight **TEEN**	**EIGH** ty
nine **TEEN**	**NINE** ty

Listen to these sentences. Write in the missing numbers as you hear them. The first one is done for you.

1. There were ___*thirteen*___ students in our class _____ days in a row.

2. I bought _____ items at the grocery store, and the bill was _____ dollars.

3. She was _____ years old in 19_____.

4. I visited Egypt in _____ _____.

5. _____ people work on the _____th floor of this building.

6. Our school library has _____ thousand books and _____ thousand magazines.

7. At five-_____, _____ of the guests had already arrived.

Listen to these sentences again, and repeat after the speaker. Be careful to use the correct stress pattern when you pronounce the numbers.

Student A: Put an X next to **one** phrase in each of the pairs in the left-hand column. Do not tell Student B which you marked. Read the phrase to Student B using the correct intonation.

Student B: Listen to the phrase that Student A reads, and put an X next to the appropriate ending from the right-hand column.

After you and your partner have completed all four items, compare your answers. Then reverse roles and repeat the exercise.

1. _____ In 1917,   _____ there was a revolution in Russia.

   _____ In 1970,   _____ Richard Nixon was the U.S. president.

2. _____ Fifteen dollars seems like   _____ a good price for that CD.

   _____ Fifty dollars seems like   _____ a fair price for front row concert seats.

3. _____ She was eighteen when   _____ she moved out of her parents' house.

   _____ She was eighty when   _____ her great grandchild was born.

4. _____ Thirteen eggs   _____ were used to make this cake.

   _____ Thirty eggs   _____ broke on the floor.

Look at this bank statement. Student B will look at the checkbook register on page 216. Ask each other questions about the bank statement and checkbook register to find two mistakes.

Greentree Bank

Monthly Statement
Account number: 2305015

Date	Description	Withdrawals	Deposits	Balance
6/13	Starting balance			460.17
6/14	Check #366	90.70		369.27
6/15	Check #368	19.13		350.34
6/17	Check #369	50.15		300.19
6/18	Deposit		730.16	1030.35
6/23	ATM—withdrawal	40.00		990.35
6/25	Check #367	17.80		972.55
6/30	Check #370	114.18		858.37

Look at this checkbook register. Student A will look at the bank statement on page 215. Ask each other questions about the checkbook register and bank statement to find two mistakes.

Check Number	Date	Description	Withdrawals	Deposits	Balance
					460.17
366	6/14	College Bookstore	90.70		369.47
367	6/15	Tempo Music	17.80		351.67
368	6/15	Electric Company	19.13		332.54
DEP	6/18	Deposit		730.16	1062.70
ATM	6/23	Debit card withdrawal	40.00		1022.70
370	6/30	BFI Telephone	114.18		908.52

The pronunciation of the *-ed*, *-s*, and *-es* endings in English depends on the last sound of the base word. The *-ed* ending is used for regular past tense verbs. The *-s* and *-es* endings are used for plural nouns and for present tense verbs. The rules are easy to learn, but it is a good idea to review voiced and voiceless sounds in Chapter 24 before starting this chapter.

Rule 1: If the base word ends in a voiced sound, use the voiced endings: /z/, /d/.

Examples:

    s**ays** /z/   ga**mes** /z/   answe**red** /d/   sa**ved** /d/

Rule 2: If the base word ends in a voiceless sound, use the voiceless endings: /s/, /t/.

Examples:

    sto**ps** /s/   ca**ts** /s/   coo**ked** /t/   wi**shed** /t/

Rule 3: If the base of the verb ends in /t/ or /d/, pronounce the past tense ending /ɪd/. This adds a syllable to the word.

Examples:

    reflec**ted** /ɪd/   exten**ded** /ɪd/

Rule 4: If the base word ends in /s/, /z/, /ʃ/, /ʒ/, /tʃ/, or /dʒ/, pronounce the *-s* ending as /ɪz/. This adds a syllable to the word.

Examples:

    busine**sses** /ɪz/   qui**zzes** /ɪz/   wi**shes** /ɪz/

    gara**ges** /ɪz/   wa**tches** /ɪz/   chan**ges** /ɪz/

A. Listen to this conversation in which a boss and an employee discuss the employee's performance at work. Write in the missing words, which have *-ed*, *-s*, and *-es* endings. The first one is done for you.

A: Let me get **(1)** ___*started*___ by telling you how much I've

(2) _____ working with you this year.

B: Thank you.

A: You've been involved in some big **(3)** _____ and you've

established a reputation for being good with **(4)** _____,

and that's important here. Now, tell me about your future career

(5) _____.

B: I've always **(6)** _____ to work in market research.

I hope there will be more opportunities for me in that area.

A: Tara tells me you got terrific **(7)** _____ to the research

you did for her, so I'm sure that can be **(8)** _____.

Now, what would you change about the past year?

B: The Simmons project really **(9)** _____ me out. There

were so many **(10)** _____! Phil says he

(11) _____ we had worked more closely on the schedule

at the very beginning, and I agree.

A: But, you know, last minute **(12)** _____ usually can't be

(13) _____.

B: Of course. But right now, one change **(14)** _____ the

project late, and that **(15)** _____ us money.

B. Listen to this list of words, and write each word in the column showing the rule for pronouncing the ending. The first one is done for you.

Rule 1 Voiced ending /d/ or /z/	Rule 2 Voiceless ending /t/ or /s/	Rules 3 and 4 Additional syllable /ɪd/ or /ɪz/
1. _____	_____	_____*started*_____
2. _____	_____	_____
3. _____	_____	_____
4. _____	_____	_____
5. _____	_____	_____
6. _____	_____	_____
7. _____	_____	_____
8. _____	_____	_____
9. _____	_____	_____
10. _____	_____	_____
11. _____	_____	_____
12. _____	_____	_____
13. _____	_____	_____
14. _____	_____	_____
15. _____	_____	_____

Listen to the words again and repeat after the speaker. Be careful to pronounce the endings correctly.

Guided Pronunciation Practice

Circle one word or phrase in each column below to make complete sentences. Then move around the classroom and ask your classmates questions to try to find someone who chose the same sentence that you did. Be careful to pronounce the endings correctly.

Example: "Liz's sister gives away coins"

/s/	Kate's	(sister)	likes	plants.
/z/	The boys'	cousin	(gives away)	(coins.)
/ɪz/	(Liz's)	uncle	wishes for	riches.

A. Practice with /s/, /z/, and /ɪz/ endings.

/s/	Kate's	sister	likes	plants.
/z/	The boys'	cousin	gives away	coins.
/ɪz/	Liz's	uncle	wishes for	riches.

B. Practice with /t/, /d/, and /ɪd/ endings.

/t/	Mom	cooked	and	chopped	the potatoes.
/d/	The chef	fried	and	boiled	the vegetables.
/ɪd/	My friends	blended	and	tasted	the food.

Guided Pronunciation Practice

C. Make your own practice. With a small group, add as many words as you can to the following chart. Then make as many sentences using *-s*, *-es*, and *-ed* endings as you can. Be sure to pronounce the endings correctly. You can make the sentences as silly or as serious as you want to.

Possessive noun	Plural noun	Regular past tense verb	Plural noun phrase
Simon's	teachers	helped	the girls.
The cat's	sons	visited	their friends.
______	______	______	______
______	______	______	______
______	______	______	______
______	______	______	______
______	______	______	______
______	______	______	______
______	______	______	______
______	______	______	______

Tell the story shown in these four pictures. With a partner, make up an ending to the story. Then practice telling the story, first in present tense, then in past tense. As you tell the story, be sure to pronounce -ed, -s, and -es endings correctly.

Chapter 42

/ʌ/ + /r/*

When /r/ follows a vowel sound in English, the /r/ makes the vowel sound different than it does alone or when it is followed by any other consonant. This change is especially strong when /r/ follows the /ə/ sound as in fath**er** or the same sound in a stressed syllable, /ʌ/, as in f**u**n, but in fact, it happens with all vowel sounds in English. To make these vowel plus /r/ sounds, curl your tongue more than you would for the vowel alone, and start saying the /r/ sound at the same time that you say the vowel sound.

In these examples, the first word has /ʌ/ or /ə/ alone; the second word has the vowel sound plus /r/. You can hear how different the vowel sounds when followed by /r/.

Examples:

   shut   sh**ir**t   ton   t**ur**n   study   st**ur**dy   tun**a**   tun**er**

*Sometimes this sound is symbolized as /ɜʳ/. In unstressed syllables, it can be symbolized as /ɚ/.

Listening Practice

A. Irma and Vern worry too much. Listen to their conversation, and write in the missing words as you hear them. The first one is done for you.

1. Vern is worried because the ___*world*___ news gets _____ every day.

2. Irma is worried about the _____ because the environment is getting _____.

3. Vern is worried that he won't _____ enough to pay for school and his rent.

4. Vern is also worried that he will get to _____ late.

5. Irma is worried that someone might steal her _____.

6. Irma is also worried because she is turning _____ next year.

7. Vern worried most about his little _____. He hopes she doesn't get _____.

8. Irma and Vern should be worrying about their _____ paper that is due on _____.

B. Listen to the vowel sounds in each word in these groups. Some words have a /ʌ/ plus /r/ sound; others have /ʌ/ only. Mark the word in each group that is different. The first one is done for you.

1. __✗__   _____   _____

2. _____   _____   _____

3 _____   _____   _____

4. _____   _____   _____

5. _____   _____   _____

6. _____   _____   _____

7. _____   _____   _____

8. _____   _____   _____

Listen to the words again, and repeat after the speaker. Be careful to pronounce the /ʌ/ + /r/ sounds correctly.

Guided Pronunciation Practice
Student A

Student A: Look at the chart below. Student B will work with the chart on page 228. Ask your partner questions to find out the occupations that are missing for the people on your chart. Your partner will ask you similar questions to find out the occupations that are missing from the chart on page 228.

Example:

Student A: What does Sherman Lerner do?

Student B: He's a barber.

Sherman Lerner	Esther Stewart	Peter McNerney
barber	postal worker	____________
Gertrude Murray	Burt Fisher	Veronica Burns
plumber	____________	bank teller
Robert Merino	Jennifer Byrd	Earl Thurston
____________	hairdresser	____________

Discuss two or more of these questions with a group of your classmates. There are many comparisons in these questions, so be sure to pronounce the *-er* endings and other vowels followed by /r/ correctly.

1. Is it bett**er** to give or to receive?

2. Which is w**or**se: being th**ir**sty or being hungry?

3. Who makes a bett**er** lead**er**: an old**er** p**er**son or a young**er** p**er**son?

4. Do you pref**er** to be f**ir**st or last?

5. Do you usually arrive at a party **ear**lier than others or lat**er**?

6. As children grow up, do their parents w**or**ry about them more or less?

7. How can you l**ear**n new w**or**ds fast**er**?

8. Which is more important: **ear**ning money or doing w**or**k you enjoy?

Guided Pronunciation Practice
Student B

Student B: Look at the chart below. Student A will work with the chart on page 226. Ask your partner questions to find out the occupations that are missing for the people on your chart. Your partner will ask you similar questions to find out the occupations that are missing from the chart on page 226.

Example:

> **Student A:** What does Sherman Lerner do?
>
> **Student B:** He's a barber.

Sh**er**man L**er**n**er**	Esth**er** Stew**ar**t	Pet**er** McN**er**ney
barb**er**	______________	carpent**er**
G**er**trude M**ur**ray	B**ur**t Fish**er**	V**er**onica B**ur**ns
______________	jewel**er**	______________
Rob**er**t M**er**ion	Jennif**er** By**r**d	**Ear**l Th**ur**ston
n**ur**se	______________	newscast**er**

English words often have several consonant sounds that are pronounced together with no vowels between them. These groups of consonants are called *consonant clusters*. In this chapter, you will practice consonant clusters at the beginning of words.

For practice with consonant clusters at the ends of words, visit the *Sound Bites* website.

Many clusters of two consonants have /s/ as the first sound.

Examples: <u>st</u>op, <u>sm</u>all, <u>sn</u>ap, <u>sl</u>ide

Other clusters have /w/, /r/, /l/, or /y/ as the second sound.

Examples: <u>tw</u>ice, <u>cr</u>y, <u>pl</u>ane, <u>cu</u>te

Be careful! The spelling of some words that start with clusters can be misleading:

Examples: <u>qu</u>ick (The cluster is pronounced /kw/.)

<u>cu</u>be (The cluster is pronounced /ky/.)

There are some clusters that have three sounds: /s/ + another cluster!

Examples: <u>str</u>ong, <u>scr</u>eam, <u>spr</u>ead

If your first language does not have consonant clusters, you may need extra practice pronouncing them. Be sure not to add a vowel sound before the cluster or between the consonants in the cluster!

A. Listen to these words, and circle the word or words that you hear. Pay special attention to which words have consonant clusters. The first one is done for you.

1. (blow)   below

2. please   police

3. twin   to win

4. friend   far end

5. brain   Bahrain

6. claps   collapse

7. trick   to Rick

8. state   estate

9. sleep   asleep

10. scream   ice cream

11. steam   esteem

12. sweat   as wet

Listen to the words again and repeat after the speaker. Be careful to pronounce the consonant clusters correctly.

B. Listen to this presentation about the life of a star. Write in the missing letters at the beginning of the word to complete the consonant clusters. The first one is done for you.

Did you know that **(1)** __*st*__ars are born, grow up, get old, and die just as living things do? The entire **(2)** _____ocess takes almost 10 billion years, but stars do go **(3)** _____ough several distinct **(4)** _____ages in their lives.

The star **(5)** _____arts out as a nebula, or a **(6)** _____oud of gases. **(7)** _____avity pulls the gases **(8)** _____oser together and they begin to heat up. As the heat and **(9)** _____essure rise, the star burns **(10)** _____ightly. At this early stage, the star's color is often **(11)** _____ue or **(12)** _____een.

When most of the hydrogen is burned, the star's heat **(13)** _____eads out, and the star becomes a larger, cooler red giant. Red giants are not very **(14)** _____able. Eventually, the outer layer of gases will **(15)** _____ow away. If the star is very heavy, it will explode in a **(16)** _____endid display of light and color called a supernova.

Lighter **(17)** _____aller stars will simply have **(18)** _____eams of gases **(19)** _____etching away from their white hot core, and the old star is then called a white **(20)** _____arf.

Look at the items on the *Things to Do* list below. You may write each item on any days that you choose. Then, ask your classmates questions about their calendars. Did any of you plan the same activity for the same day?

Things To Do

1. **dr**ive **Gr**andma to the **gr**ocery **st**ore
2. **qu**it **sm**oking
3. **pr**actice **sp**eaking **Sp**anish
4. **sw**im **thr**ee miles
5. **pl**ay **sp**orts after **sch**ool
6. **pl**an a **c**lass **pr**oject
7. shop for **cl**othes at the **St**ate **Str**eet mall
8. **cl**ean house:
   - **sw**eep the **fl**oor
   - **scr**ub the **st**ove
   - take out the **tr**ash

April
Sunday *April 1ˢᵗ*
Saturday *April 2ⁿᵈ*
Monday *April 3ʳᵈ*
Tuesday *April 4ᵗʰ*
Wednesday *April 5ᵗʰ*
Thursday *April 6ᵗʰ*
Friday *April 7ᵗʰ*
Sunday *April 8ᵗʰ*
Saturday *April 9ᵗʰ*

Add a word containing the same consonant cluster as the first word in each list below. With a partner, choose 10 or more words from the lists and create a story or a dialog using these words.

/bl/	/br/	/fr/	/gl/
black	bring	free	glass
_____	_____	_____	_____

/kl/	/kw/	/pl/	/pr/
clean	quiet	play	price
_____	_____	_____	_____

/sl/	/sm/	/st/	/thr/
slow	smell	step	through
_____	_____	_____	_____

/tw/	/str/	/scr/	/spr/
twelve	straight	scrape	spring
_____	_____	_____	_____

_____

_____

_____

_____

_____

_____

_____

Chapter 44

Adjustments in Fast Speech

In fast speech, some English words sound quite different from the way they sound in slow speech. In Chapter 3 you learned about the importance of rhythm in English. English speakers make adjustments in fast speech to maintain this rhythm.

Adjustment 1: /h/ Deletion
The sound /h/ is often not pronounced when it is at the beginning of function words such as

    H̶e   H̶is   H̶er   H̶im   H̶ave   H̶as   H̶ad

Example:

    should **h**ave *sounds like* shoulda   did **he** *sounds like* didee

Adjustment 2: *and*, *or*, and *of*
These words are pronounced very quickly. *And* and *or* are pronounced as just one sound.

    and *sounds like* n   **or** *sounds like* r

Of is pronounced /ə/ before a consonant but /əv/ before a vowel.

    waste **of** time *sounds like* waste a time
    most **of** us *sounds like* most uv us

Adjustment 3: Deleted Sounds
Unstressed vowels in some words are not pronounced at all. Sometimes an entire syllable is dropped!

Examples:

    fav**o**rite *sounds like* fav'rite   proba**b**ly *sounds like* prob'bly
    gen**e**ral *sounds like* gen'ral   s**u**ppose *sounds like* s'pose
    mem**o**ry *sounds like* mem'ry   **be**cause *sounds like* 'cause

A more complete list of words that often have deleted syllables is on the *Sound Bites* website.

A. Each of these sentences contains at least one example of the adjustments in fast speech that are described in this chapter. Listen to each sentence, and circle *formal* if the sentence is pronounced formally without any adjustments. Circle *informal* if the sentence is pronounced informally using one or more adjustments. The first one is done for you.

1. Formal   (Informal)

2. Formal   Informal

3. Formal   Informal

4. Formal   Informal

5. Formal   Informal

6. Formal   Informal

7. Formal   Informal

8. Formal   Informal

9. Formal   Informal

10. Formal   Informal

B. Listen to this dialog and pay attention to the adjustments that have been marked.

A: Hi there.

B: Hi. Did he call?

A: No, he didn't call, **and** he probably won't.

  *(n above **and**)*

B: But he told me he'd call.

A: Of course he did. People practically always say they'll call after a first date, **and** they generally don't.

  *(n above **and**)*

B: Why not?

A: I don't know. Maybe because he has got a bad memory... **or** maybe because he doesn't want to seem too eager — like he's thinking about you **all of the** time.

  *(r above **or**)*

  *(all a the above **all of the**)*

B: If I say I'll call, I do. I should have asked him for his number. We had such a nice evening together!

A: Well, **most of us** don't expect a call the next day, **and** I think it's a **waste of time** to sit by the phone.

  *(most uv us above **most of us**)*

  *(n above **and**)*

  *(waste a time above **waste of time**)*

The phone rings.

B: I'll get it!

With a partner, practice reading the dialog in Listening Practice Exercise B. Read the dialog several times until you can pronounce the adjustments fluently.

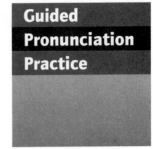

Guided Pronunciation Practice

Write a dialog using as many words and phrases from this chapter as you can. Mark the adjustments and read the dialog with a partner or on a cassette tape. Try to say the adjustments as a native speaker would in fast informal speech.

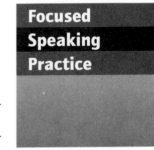

Focused Speaking Practice

_____

_____

_____

_____

_____

_____

_____

_____

_____

Chapter 45

More Adjustments in Fast Speech

In fast speech, the /t/ and /d/ sounds sometimes change when they are next to other sounds.

Adjustment 1: /n/ + /t/ *sounds like* /n/

When /t/ follows /n/, often the /t/ is not pronounced.

Examples:

cen**t**er *sounds like* cenner	can'**t** we *sounds like* can we[1]
going **to** *sounds like* gonna	wan**t to** *sounds like* wanna[2]

Adjustment 2: /t/ Flap

When /t/ is between a stressed vowel and either an unstressed vowel or sometimes an /l/ sound,[3] it is pronounced with a quick tap of the tongue against the teeth. It sounds more like /d/ than /t/.

Examples:

wa**t**er *sounds like* wadder	li**tt**le *sounds like* liddle
ge**t** in *sounds like* ged in	

Adjustment 3: /t/ or /d/ + /y/

When /t/ is followed by /y/, together they sound like /tʃ/.
When /d/ is followed by /y/, together they sound like /dʒ/.

Examples:

don'**t you** *sounds like* doncha	ge**t you** *sounds like* getcha
di**d you** *sounds like* didja	woul**d you** *sounds like* wouldja

[1]See Chapter 38 for practice with *can* and *can't*.
[2]See Chapter 39 to learn about consonant linking.
[3]Sometimes /l/ can be a syllable all by itself without a vowel sound. When /t/ comes between a stressed vowel and this syllabic /l/, it is pronounced as a flap.

A. Each of these sentences contains at least one example of the adjustments in fast speech that are described in this chapter. Listen to each sentence, and circle *formal* if the sentence is pronounced formally without any adjustments. Circle *informal* if the sentence is pronounced informally using one or more adjustments. The first one is done for you.

1. (Formal)   Informal

2. Formal   Informal

3. Formal   Informal

4. Formal   Informal

5. Formal   Informal

6. Formal   Informal

7. Formal   Informal

8. Formal   Informal

9. Formal   Informal

10. Formal   Informal

B. Listen to this dialog, and pay attention to the adjustments that have been marked.

        wanna
A: I **want to** return this TV.

           didja
B: When **did you** buy it?

    liddle
A: A **little** over a week ago.

          gonna   **needjer**   **gotta**
B: OK. I'm **going to need your** receipt, and you've **got to** fill in this form.

            ged a bedder
A: I'd like to **get a better** model, if that's OK.

                    twenny
B: Oh. Of course. There's a sale on **twenty**-inch screen TVs this

         plenny   **dontcha**
week. There are **plenty** of choices. Why **don't you** pick out

 whatcha
what you want first?

                      pud it
A: What should I do with this one? Should I **put it** back on the shelf?

                    cenner   **counner**
B: You can leave it here in the **center** of the **counter**.

With a partner, practice reading the dialog in Listening Practice Exercise B. Read the dialog several times until you can pronounce the adjustments fluently.

Guided Pronunciation Practice

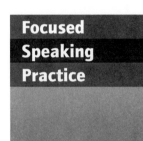

Write a dialog using as many words and phrases from this chapter as you can. Mark the adjustments and read the dialog with a partner or on a cassette tape. Try to say the adjustments as a native speaker would in fast informal speech.

Focused Speaking Practice

_____

_____

_____

_____

_____

_____

_____

_____

_____